Getting the
BLUES

Getting the
BLUES

What Blues Music Teaches Us about
Suffering and Salvation

STEPHEN J. NICHOLS

Brazos Press

a division of Baker Publishing Group
Grand Rapids, Michigan

Published by Brazos Press
a division of Baker Publishing Group
P.O. Box 6287, Grand Rapids, MI 49516–6287
www.brazospress.com

Printed in the United States of America

Library of Congress Cataloging-in-Publication Data
Nichols, Stephen J., 1970–
        Getting the blues : what blues music teaches us about suffering and salvation
    / Stephen J. Nichols.
            p.   cm.
        Includes bibliographical references.
        ISBN 978-1-58743-212-5 (pbk.)
        1. Blues (Music)—Religious aspects. 2. Blues (Music)—History and criticism.
    I. Title.
    ML3921.8.B68N53 2008
    781.643'11—dc22   2008019718

To the Memory of

Charley Patton, 1891–1934,

Bluesman and Preacher

Contents

Contents

Acknowledgments

One spiritual tells you that you've got to go through the lonesome valley, a metaphor for death, alone. Another tells you that *we* are climbing Jacob's ladder. Writing a book isn't exactly like a near-death experience but, like the spirituals say, it can be an odd mix of solitude and community. As for the latter, there are many people that I'd like to thank for helping me navigate this valley of the blues.

Nick Spitzer and his NPR program, "American Routes," is likely more responsible for this book than anyone or anything else. He introduced me to the blues and to the writings of Alan Lomax. I'm also grateful to Clarence Christian, who led a National Collegiate Honors Council trek through Memphis and into the Delta. Eric Brandt once again plied his skills as a researcher, supplying reams of lyrics at just the right time. Steve Turner offered quite helpful advice in the early stages and a steady stream of encouragement along the way. Tom Douglas took a long enough break from writing hit songs for Tim McGraw to read the manuscript and, in his characteristic grace, cheer me on. I knew Rodney Clapp was the ideal editor for this book when he emailed me as he happened to be staying at the same Texas hotel where Robert Johnson made his recordings. Once again I am grateful to my colleagues and the administrators at Lancaster Bible College. They are quick to offer support and slow to complain about the howling music emanating from my office.

Finally I am grateful to my wife, Heidi. She picked up the slack as I went off into the lonesome valley of writing, proved a great sounding board as I would emerge from time to time to try out ideas and paragraphs, and (most importantly?) offered no criticism whatsoever as I added a few rows to my CD collection. She's a dream.

"Where the Southern Crosses the Dog," Moorehead, Mississippi, the site where the Southern Railway line crosses the Yazoo Delta Railway (called the Yellow Dog).

Prelude

Learning to Hear the Blues

One late January, I was having dinner with friends. The conversation inevitably turned to football. Having severely limited knowledge on that topic, I thought I'd be better off changing the subject, so I interjected a story from a book I was reading at the time, Alan Lomax's saga of the Mississippi Delta, *The Land Where the Blues Began*. The timing could not have been worse, and the particular story that I chose—concerning the squalid conditions of workers in the levee camps along the Mississippi river—could not have been more ill suited for dinner conversation. Even so, I had not anticipated the response, which came quickly: "Why are you reading that book?" I had no good answer. I simply muttered something like "It provides a context for listening to the blues." I failed to convince my companions.

I have since given a great deal of thought to that question. In fact, I have extended the question beyond the unsavory episodes of Lomax's book. Why read stories and listen to songs of tragedy and loss, despair and alienation? Why look at the darker side of life? The answer I wish I had given that night, and the answer I'm only beginning to appreciate, is this: I read and listen to the stories of these less-than-pleasant elements of life in order to understand, so that I can hear and see that which I don't always hear and see.

By just about any standard, my upbringing and current status, hovering around middle-class American culture, has made my life far simpler than the lives of hosts of my fellow human beings throughout our common history. This is not to minimize the challenges and trials, ordeals and sufferings of those in my family or circle of friends, or those of us who are (mostly white) suburban Americans. Still, we enjoy many blessings not experienced by previous generations or by all peoples. I'm not lamenting these blessings—simply recognizing that sometimes they come at a price. They can cause us to miss some vital elements of life.

We American evangelicals are as likely as anybody else to be missing something when it comes to a fuller view of life and humanity. In addition, we just might be overlooking something in the pages of scripture. C. S. Lewis wrote hauntingly of Narnia, where it was always winter and never Christmas. For many American evangelicals, life is like always having spring and summer without winter or fall. Or always Easter and never Good Friday. Not everything, however—in life or in the Bible—plays out in a major key.

This book attempts a theology in a minor key, a theology that lingers, however uncomfortably, over Good Friday. It takes its cue from the blues, harmonizing narratives of scripture with narratives of the Mississippi Delta, the land of cotton fields and cypress swamps and the moaning slide guitar. I am not a musician, but a theologian, and so I offer a theological interpretation of the blues. Cambridge theologian Jeremy Begbie has argued for music's intrinsic ability to teach theology. As an improvisation on Begbie's thesis, I take the blues to be intrinsically suited to teach a particular theology, a theology in a minor key.

This is not to suggest that a theology in a minor key—or the blues, for that matter—sounds out utter despair like the torrents of a spinning hurricane. A theology in a minor key is no mere existential scream. In fact, a theology in a minor key sounds a rather hopeful melody. Good Friday yearns for Easter, and eventually Easter comes. Blues singers, even when groaning about the worst of times, know to cry out for mercy; they know that, despite appearances, Sunday's coming.

My theological interpretation of the blues essentially becomes christological. Ralph C. Wood rightfully titled his book on one of the South's most engaging writers *Flannery O'Connor and the Christ-Haunted South*. Though working in a different medium and coming from a different socioeconomic place than O'Connor, blues men and women worked in the same "Christ-haunted" South. Well before the blues showed up, Christ inhabited Negro spirituals. According to "Daniel Saw the Stone," Christ was the stone cut from the mountain without hands. He was the deliverer, the one who could make a way out of nowhere. He was the good shepherd, restoring his lost sheep. When the blues came around, Christ remained. He bore the curse, he suffered exile and abandonment, he was the Man of Sorrows. The blues, like the writings of Flannery O'Conner, need not mention him in every line or in every song, but he haunts the music just the same. At the end of the day, he resolves the conflict churning throughout the blues, the conflict that keeps the music surging like the floodwaters of the Mississippi River. Christ resolves the conflict precisely because he enters the conflict itself. He is Emmanuel, God with us, which ultimately makes him God for us.

In his delightful book *The Smell of Sawdust*, Richard Mouw recalls ever-present memories of the songs and hymns of his fundamentalist background. Similar memories are mine as well. I remember an exasperated Sunday-school teacher as we kids did mocking motions to "I'll Fly Away." With its catchy tune and heavenward look, the song held little sway over me.

All I wanted to do was flap my arms like a bird. My life was not hard or sad; it was enjoyable and full of good things and protection and warmth and loving people.

But I can now imagine a congregation in Alan Lomax's Mississippi Delta, a congregation of sharecroppers and slave descendants in the 1930s. A congregation of men who must call the plantation owner's ten-year-old son Mister, while he calls them Boy. A congregation of orphaned children and widowed women and abandoned wives and disillusioned men. A congregation of men and women of sorrows. A congregation of human beings barely clinging to their humanity. And they're singing "I'll Fly Away" in the tiny clapboard church, and they're clapping and stomping out the beat. And they're waiting—waiting for some glad day when they cross the golden shore, waiting for Sunday to come, waiting for the Man of Sorrows whose mercy knows no bounds.

This book is their story. It will never be mine, and I can never pretend that it will be. But I can listen, and I can try to understand. They and the blues gave me back "I'll Fly Away." Both of them can give me and us so much more if we listen. As we listen we also hear the story of the Man of Sorrows, the One who inhabits the world of the blues, Emmanuel who longs to sing the song of Zion with his people.

Barn on Stovall Plantation,
home of Muddy Waters, near Clarksdale, Mississippi.

1

What Hath Mississippi to Do with Jerusalem?

A Theologian Explores the World of the Blues

Blues is the roots, everything else is the fruits.

Willie Dixon

In the early years of the third century, the church father Tertullian quipped, "What hath Athens to do with Jerusalem?" His question articulated the challenge that faced the church in his day and throughout the centuries since then. What relationship does the church—do Christians— have with culture? For Tertullian, this question centered on the relationship between philosophy—symbolized by Athens, the home of Socrates and Plato—and faith, whose home was the holy city of Jerusalem. Tertullian answers his rhetorical question with a resounding "Nothing!" Philosophy is dangerous, he believes. Heretics get their weapons from philosophers. Besides, he adds, it is entirely unnecessary. What need have we for curiosity since we have Christ? A good question—but I can't help thinking that Tertullian came up with the wrong answer.[1]

A Christianity closed up in itself might be safe from heresy. For that matter, a life without curiosity might be safe. But such a Christianity and such a life might also be stifling and suffocating. Further, it's worth considering the impact of Tertullian's view on apologetics. His unengaged approach to life and culture leaves the Christian with little ground in common with the non-Christian. The withdrawal from the world he endorses stymies finding inroads and connections for the gospel. The apologetics argument, however, stops short of what may be the most damning indictment of Tertullian. His approach cuts us off from learning anything from others who just might have something to teach us. Engaging culture is a two-way street; we find common ground to speak the gospel to others, and from others we gain better understanding of the gospel. All of which is to say that Mississippi has a lot to do with Jerusalem.

I prefer Dietrich Bonhoeffer's approach to the question of the Christian and culture. He told us, from his prison cell at Tegel, that Christ calls us to "worldliness," to be worldly disciples He does not mean for us to be accommodated to the world or merged or lost in it. Instead, Bonhoeffer calls us to be fully engaged, to be incarnational, to be aware. Such awareness helps us see what we would otherwise, due to our limited experiences, prejudices, and biases, likely miss. Mississippi, specifically the Mississippi Delta, the home of the blues, can help those of us who live in Jerusalem to be more aware. As Athens is giving way to Mississippi, perhaps Jerusalem is giving way to Wheaton or to Colorado Springs—the former and more recent homes of the American evangelical establishment. There have been plenty of studies of Wheaton and Colorado Springs and of all the other centers of American

"Black, Blue, & White:
Gettin' the Blues"

Johnny Cash, did you get the blues in Memphis?

Or did you get the blues when Jack died and you
    were fishin'
    And he told you to go on ahead and it'd be
    alright?

Or did you get the blues when you realized
    June wasn't so far out of reach after all
    And maybe she loved you more than you loved
    her?

Did you get the blues in Memphis when you
    walked the streets
    And you couldn't pay the rent?

Did you learn your rhythm watching the black
    boys shinin' shoes?
    Or did you learn your rhythm pickin' the cotton
    and puttin' it in the sack?
    Or did you learn it from those church songs in
    your mama's hymn book?

Tell us, Johnny Cash, did you get the blues in
    Memphis
    pickin' your guitar
    for Sam Phillips
    while the people walked by
    and looked in the window
    and thought
    just another white boy
    in from the fields
    thinkin' he's gonna sell some records?

                     SJN

evangelical thought, but theologians have attempted fewer forays into Mississippi. Book-length treatments include James Cone's *Spirituals and the Blues* and Jon Michael Spencer's *Blues and Evil*. In the latter Spencer coins the term *theomusicologist*, putting a twist on the category of ethnomusicology and endorsing the historical, scientific, cultural, and *theological* study of music. A theomusicology of the blues follows in the chapters below. This chapter proceeds with the elusive task of defining our terms and laying out the terrain.[2]

Getting the Blues

What is the blues? The song "Dallas Blues" tells us, "The blues ain't nothing but a good man feeling bad." Muddy Waters, the prince of the Delta blues, said that the blues has to do with a woman leaving a man, and not under the best of circumstances. A humorous attempt at defining the blues establishes its criteria:. traveling by Greyhound counts, but not traveling by plane; driving Chevys, Fords, broken-down trucks, and an occasional Cadillac qualifies, but driving Volvos and BMWs doesn't. The blues may be found in such places as a jailhouse, morgue, room with an empty bed, back highway, or the bottom of an empty bottle, but not at Nordstrom's, the mall, a gallery opening, or the golf course. This is the nonmusical approach to defining the blues, what *The New Grove Dictionary of Music and Musicians* refers to as defining the blues as a "state of mind." That's not to dismiss it, for *Grove's* adds that this is its "most important extra-musical meaning." Blues is a feeling, and a particularly low, if not moribund, one.[3]

Alternatively, we could get technical in our definition. The blues is a particular type of music, the twelve-bar tune being the most popular, with distinctive flatted third and seventh notes on the major scale, producing the "blue note," a term coined by W. C. Handy and known nontechnically as that

troubling "minor-key" sound. The twelve-bar tune gives structure to the improvisations of the blues musicians who, though
skilled, rarely were able to read music. The twelve-bar tune
could accommodate modification as eight- and sixteen-bar
tunes, as well. A technical pattern could be ascribed to the
lyrics set to the twelve-bar tunes: three-line verses of four
bars each. The second line repeats the first, and the third is
a response or an answer. Consider Blind Lemon Jefferson's
1927 recording of an often-heard blues song:

> I'm sittin' here thinkin' will a matchbox hold my
>   clothes
> I'm sittin' here thinkin' will a matchbox hold my
>   clothes
> Ain't got so many matches, but I sure got a long way
>   to go.

Or there's the example that appeared with various modifica-
tions in many a blues artist's repertoire:

> I'm a po' boy, long way from home,
> I'm a po' boy, long way from home,
> I'm a po' boy, ain't got nowhere to roam.

Some speculate that the first line was repeated to give the
musician time to think about the third, since many of these
songs were made up as they went along.

Musical and lyrical conventions, however, are meant to be
broken. The basic blues lyrical format more often than not
met with modification. Just as seasoned writers drift from the
basic-essay format dutifully learned in English composition
courses, the more skillful musicians quickly find their own
way both musically and lyrically.[4]

That said, the blues, and especially the early Delta blues,
forms a distinct genre. Rhythmic and haunting as it emanates
from the hollows of the Mississippi Delta, it comes punctuated with the pain of the sharecropper, the levee worker, the

railroad worker, the dock shoreman, or the inmate at a hell-hole like Parchman Prison—the prison farm that historians have called an early-1900s form of slavery. Outsiders had more idyllic perspectives, as seen in promotional literature of the Delta by the Illinois Central Railroad. It likened the Delta of the 1910s to the pre–Civil War slave plantations: "Nowhere in Mississippi have antebellum conditions of land holding been so nearly preserved as in the Delta." Then, like the best of advertising, it added this spin: "The Negro is naturally gregarious in instinct, and is never so happy as when massed together in large numbers, as on the Delta plantations." This ad copy was written by those, presumably, whose connection to the Delta consisted of looking at it out the railroad car windows. For those living in the Delta, things looked different. The music of this region, like its musicians, would come of age and leave its roots, heading north to the big city. In Chicago, guitars were plugged in and the blues were electrified. Seductive guitar riffs replaced harmonica ballads. The pain of survival in the Delta would be exchanged for the promise of success in the city.[5]

In the 1960s the blues met white suburbanite teenagers, a demographic with discretionary cash. Had Elvis and Johnny Cash and Jerry Lee Lewis and Roy Orbison—record producer Sam Phillips's cadre—won over white audiences to black rhythms? The Rolling Stones, taking their name from a Muddy Waters line, and Eric Clapton, claiming he owes everything to the legacy of Robert Johnson, have furthered this route of the blues. The blues had a baby, the saying goes, and they named it rock 'n' roll. Willie Dixon, himself coming from the Delta, put it more expansively, "Blues is the roots, and everything else is the fruits."

Muddy Waters personifies this transmigration of the blues. Waters was discovered by Alan Lomax, the ethnomusicologist who recorded disc after disc for the Library of Congress, preserving a music and a culture that otherwise would have been lost. Lomax was looking for the sound of Robert Johnson, one of the blues' most enigmatic founding fathers. But Lomax was too late, for Johnson had already died, presumably poisoned. Lomax did find Johnson's musical child on the Stovall plantation in Clarksdale, Mississippi. Born McKinley Morganfield, he was nicknamed Muddy Waters for his inability to steer clear of creeks near his family's home. He spent his years picking cotton, usually for fifty cents a day, and humming on his harmonica or strumming a guitar. Looking out the back door of his home, he saw miles of cotton fields; out the front, across the dirt road, stretched the cypress swamps. When he turned left on that dirt road, he went to the mansion house and the barns; when he turned right he would eventually come to the town and the commissary with the porch where he played his music during the day. Further into town was the juke joint where he played by night. In 1941, Waters made his first recording when Alan Lomax pulled his equipment from the trunk of his car. Two years later, Muddy Waters hitched a ride into Clarksdale, purchased a train ticket from the "colored window," and waited for the northbound train to Chicago. After his initial success, Waters reigned supreme at Chess Records studio. The 1950s were his, with such hits as "I Can't Be Satisfied" and "Hoochie Coochie Man." Muddy Waters's tours took him all over America and overseas.[6]

All this came to a man raised by his grandmother in a cypress shack with a tin roof. The blues had come of age. The blues and jazz festivals, album reissues, and concert tours—not to mention Eric Clapton's "Me and Mr. Johnson," Martin Scorsese's *The Blues* PBS series, and Ken Burns's PBS series *Jazz: A History of America's Music*—have all given the blues a prominence, and a market share, it had never dreamed possible. This book, while looking at the full life cycle of the blues, is more interested in the blues Muddy Waters left behind as he headed north. It's more interested in the blues of the 1910s through the 1930s, the years that led up to his singing "I Be's Troubled" for Alan Lomax in 1941. It's about the Delta blues and the culture that gave the blues its life.

Poet Langston Hughes made a migration similar to that of Muddy Waters. Raised in Missouri and Kansas, he moved to the outskirts of Chicago before studying at Columbia University in New York City. He was all the while determined to find his roots in the Mississippi Delta. His quest was fortuitous, producing his poem "The Negro Speaks of Rivers," before he reached his twentieth birthday. The mighty Mississippi, its bosom turning "golden brown" in the sunset, flowed through his "veins like blood." It made him who he was. His soul was deeper, fuller, as he connected with his past. Forging links to his heritage, he found ballast throughout his own experiences of being ostracized and standing on the receiving end of racist aggression. He was made strong by his solidarity with the suffering of his past. His piece on the fictional Roy Williams in his collection of stories published as *The Ways of White Folks* (1934) thinly veils autobiography. Roy had been to New York. Roy had been trained on the piano and was a world-class musician, landing a European tour. Roy was beaten and then lynched outside of Hopkinsville, Missouri. His crime? Stopping to talk with a white woman on the street. As Hughes puts it in his poem *The Negro Speaks of Rivers*, "I've known rivers: Ancient, dusky rivers. My soul has grown deep like the rivers."[7]

Langston Hughes and Muddy Waters and a host of yet-to-be-considered artists may not be a direct part of the past of many of us, *us* meaning typically white, middle-class, suburban American evangelicals. For *us,* the experience of Mississippi Delta sharecroppers is as distant and foggy as the faded black-and-white photo montage of it on a PBS documentary. But that doesn't mean that we can't learn from it, or that we can't learn something about our theology from it. In fact, because it is so distant from us, what we can learn from it is all the more urgent.

Having sketched an outline and definition of the blues, we next need to understand the land from whence it came: the Mississippi Delta, what James Cobb has called "the most Southern place on earth."[8]

Lost Delta, Still Lost

We loaded the vans and headed south on Highway 61. I had been with a group in Memphis, a faculty institute on exploring blues terrains, sponsored by the National Collegiate Honors Council. Having trekked the streets of Memphis, we were now going into the Mississippi Delta, the place of myth and legend. In fact, it's not a delta. It is far—a couple hundred miles—from the mouth of the river. It's not even technically the Mississippi Delta, as it is bordered on the east by the Yazoo River. So we went south into the Yazoo-Mississippi alluvial plain, section 2312 of the Mississippi River as declared by the Army Corps of Engineers. Something told me my quest to uncover legend and myth, looking for the lost Mississippi Delta of blues icons Robert Johnson, Son House, and Muddy Waters, would not be all that I had imagined. When we passed by the towering casinos blocking the sun at Tunica, I knew this trip would not measure up. Some things are better left in the imagination; reality has a way of tarnishing the ideal. Robert Gordon and Bruce Nemerov have published a book entitled *Lost Delta Found*. For me, the lost Delta remains lost.[9]

That the Delta may be lost does not detract from its presence in the past. The graves (Robert Johnson has three), the old broken-down juke-joints, the railroad tracks, the dilapidated plantation shacks all quietly testify to a previous era. This era and this region produced one of the most significant accomplishments in American music. No less than the redoubtable *New Grove Dictionary of Music and Musicians* states that blues is "the most extensively recorded of all music types." Others have dubbed it America's only truly indigenous music form. When the 1990 release of *The Complete Recordings*, by Robert Johnson, sold over 500,000 copies, no one could deny the blues its rightful place. What is it about the Delta that gave the blues its life?

Clifford Geertz has spoken of "thick descriptions" in the process of understanding cultures, referring to the multiple layers that constitute culture and that need to be understood in order to interpret it. Delta life invites such a thick description. There's geography, the cotton fields that stretch for miles, the cypress swamps, and the rivers. There's the plantation mansion, and there are the plantation shacks. There are cotton bins and cotton gins. There are steamboats and railroads. There's the juke joint, the place of letting loose on Saturday night. And there's the church, the place of confession on Sunday morning. There's the food. There's the heat; Bobby Blue Bland, who picked cotton in the Delta before he sang the blues in Memphis and before he toured the world with B. B. King, said of his learning to sing in the cotton fields, "You'd sing to take the heat off you." These descriptions merit exploration beneath the surface.[10]

First, there was poverty and exploitation. Though the Delta was rich in soil and water resources, not all the inhabitants equally shared in the wealth. There were the planters, who were white, and the sharecroppers, mostly but not exclusively black. Some of the region lay largely uninhabited prior to the end of the nineteenth century, though many of the Delta's plantations predated the Civil War. By the early decades of the twentieth century, many more large plantations, dotted by the crude sharecropper cabins, filled the Delta, creating what John C. Willis has termed "the plantation empire." In these decades before the levees were built, the Mississippi River's regular flooding had deposited rich soils all along its banks in the region, making it a fertile alluvial plain. One may still encounter five-foot thicknesses of soil before hitting rock. The summer heat would regularly exceed a hundred degrees, and while most crops can't survive such a scorching sun, cotton thrives under it. In the Delta, cotton became king, complete with its subordinated noble and peasant classes. In the days before machines, sharecroppers picked cotton in the heat, barehanded and hunched over, lugging the long cotton bag behind. To pass the time, they sang. Ironically, the machines that one day saved them from such excruciating work led to their downfall. When the tractors and the harvesters rolled out on to the field, there was no longer any need for share-croppers, triggering a great migration. No longer able to eke out even a subsistence level of life, they, in the words of Johnny Cash, a cotton picker from Dyess, Arkansas, "rambled north" and "rambled east." They took their music with them.[11]

It's not just the hard work and the economic and racial exploitation that account for the blues. Similarly harsh exploitation happened elsewhere and at the same time in America, such as that of the (mostly) Irish miners in the anthracite coal regions of northeastern Pennsylvania, giving rise to the legendary "Molly Maguires" and their rebellion. What may account for the difference in the Delta and the creation of the blues is the particular past of the sharecroppers in the Delta. They were the first or second generation of freed slaves, counting not a few surviving former slaves among the elderly. Slavery, for them, was not a distant past. In the W. C. Handy House Museum on Beale Street in Memphis—it was relocated there from its original site a few blocks away—there is a picture of a slave ship, underscoring for those who visit the house of the "Father of the Blues" that the blues ultimately comes from slavery. B. B. King's "Why I Sing the Blues" (1956) eventually gives the answer to his self-directed question: slavery. Yet it's not just slavery as an institution that contributes to the blues: it's the *music* of slavery, the spirituals.[12]

In *The Spirituals and the Blues,* James Cone debunks the thesis that while the spirituals are church music, the blues is the devil's music. In some ways, Cone readily admits, the disjuncture is legitimate. For instance, Son House was confronted with a crossroads decision: Should he take up the guitar and be a bluesman, or should he pick up his Bible and be a preacher? He chose the former, but he sang about the latter in "Preachin' Blues." Cone quickly points out how overdrawn the disjuncture is and argues instead for a symbiosis.[13]

The spirituals provided the blues artists with the musical experience to create their art, as well as the content from which

29

to write their lyrics. The spirituals were filled with hope and longing, all the while facing head-on the realities of sin and the harshness of life. Faulkner titled his work on the conflicts in the Delta *Go Down, Moses* (1942), during the same decades as the birth of the blues. Through the spirituals, the people of the Delta had become one with the grand story of redemption in Exodus. They had appropriated it so often that it had become their story. Blues artists also appropriated the themes of exile and bondage (sin) set against hope (redemption) throughout their music. "They call it stormy Monday," and, the song continues, "Tuesday's just as bad, Wednesday's even worse, Thursday's awfully sad." But then "Sunday I go to church where I kneel down to pray," adding, as if taking a line from *The Book of Common Prayer,* "Lord have mercy, Lord have mercy on me." The blues artists may have left the church, but the church, and especially the spirituals, hadn't left them.[14]

The exploitation and hard life of the sharecroppers, the not-nearly-distant-enough memories of slavery, and the echoing of the spirituals throughout the Yazoo-Mississippi Delta all conspired to create the blues. No one knows for sure who first sang the blues, but thanks to an official proclamation of Congress, we do know when the blues were discovered. On February 1, 2003, Congress passed a Senate resolution that 2003 be named the "Year of the Blues," commemorating the hundredth anniversary of its discovery by W. C. Handy. A ragtime bandleader, Handy was sitting on the train platform in Tutwiler, Mississippi, waiting to travel to his next engagement. Next to him, a sharecropper with a guitar, whom Handy identifies only as a "ragged Negro," began strumming the twelve-bar tune chords and singing the three-line structure that would come to be called the blues. In this version it's an AAA structure, not the typical AAB pattern:

> I'm goin' where the Southern cross the Dog,
> I'm goin' where the Southern cross the Dog,
> I'm goin' where the Southern cross the Dog.

Though a simple line (referring to two railroad lines), it manages to portray the depth of the blues in its expression of restlessness. The train platform where this discovery took place is long gone, yet another victim in the lost Delta. A few yards from where it once stood is a mural depicting the scene of Handy listening to his anonymous musician with guitar in hand. The ideal does not tarnish the real.[15]

Why I Wear Black: Theology in a Minor Key

The blues artists were not theologians, unless you want to count Son House's brief stint at preaching. Yet they imbibed a culture that was deeply and astutely theological, and they knew a storyline that began with sin and the fall, followed a road of redemption, and ended at a place of justice and peace and choruses of angels. To be sure, sometimes the blues artists got stuck in the beginning, at sin and the fall, and too often they wandered far off the road of redemption. But the gospel story was always there, and if you listen closely to the music, you can surely hear it. In fact, listening to the blues apart from its theology misses the blues altogether.

An illustrative example that is seemingly disparate from the blues is found in a recent movie on Johnny Cash. The remarkable thing about the film is that *Walk the Line*, with Joaquin Phoenix as Johnny Cash and Reese Witherspoon as June Carter, actually lived up to the hype of *The Wall Street Journal* ("Brilliant. Masterful.") and Roger Ebert ("The music is great, the drama is great, the writing is great, the performances are great."). It is a movie worthy of its subject and worthy of its praise. Punctuated with renditions of some of the best popular music of the second half of the twentieth century, the drama unfolds with intensity and depth. It even has a happy ending, but not a typical Hollywood one; its ending didn't come cheaply, and the movie (thankfully) sidestepped flaccid sentimentalism.

For all its merits, the movie suffers a fatal flaw. The rebel, the outlaw, the Man in Black, was, as he once put it, "a Christian, as I have been all my life."[16] You don't get Johnny Cash without religion. Hints are there in the film, such as when he and June hesitate as they enter a country church after his first drug rehab. But the film didn't nearly do justice to religion in Cash's life. Its let-down scene was the unprecedented Folsom Prison concert on January 13, 1968, a scene pivotally used to introduce the movie and then returned to near the end. The movie portrays the climax of the concert with Cash belting out "Cocaine Blues" in a glass-smashing, warden-bashing, hard-driving way. No doubt, the Folsom prisoners thought it a highlight. Chalk the glass-smashing up to drama, since during the real concert he had a tin cup. But otherwise the scene is gritty and authentic. June Carter would later say that the prisoners liked Johnny Cash so much because they knew he was the real thing. And, in truth, he had been behind bars (if only for a few days and nights). But in the real concert that night, the part of the outlaw was trumped by the part of the preacher. The concert's true climax came when Johnny Cash reached over the platform and shook the hand of inmate Glen Sherley, before singing Sherley's song "Greystone Chapel."

Glen Sherley was writing and recording songs while doing time at Folsom, one of California's most notorious maximum security prisons. The night before the concert, the chaplain told Johnny Cash he should listen to a tape he'd brought along. Someone produced a tape recorder, and they all listened silently:

> There's a greystone chapel here at Folsom Prison,
> A house of worship in this den of sin.
> You wouldn't think that God had a place here at
>   Folsom,
> But he saved the souls of many lost men.

And then the chorus:

> Inside the walls of prison my body may be,
> But my Lord has set my soul free.

Cash spent the rest of the night learning Sherley's "Greystone Chapel." He and his band played the song for the first time the next day. He picked it to close the concert.[17] Even without religion, the Folsom Prison scene in *Walk the Line* is one of its most powerful. If the scene had included religion, as had truly been the case, it could have been explosive.

Admittedly, Johnny Cash may appear out of place in a discussion of the blues. He's more country music than blues. And he's white.

"No Black. No White. Just Blues." I first heard this blues motto when Nick Spitzer, host of NPR's *American Routes* program of indigenous American music, read the words off the shirt worn by that day's studio guest, Louisiana bluesman Lazy Lester. Cash and the motto remind us that the blues ultimately has no racial divide. The blues can, however, be a *bridge across* a racial divide if, at the very least, as far as the historical Delta blues is concerned, it helps us understand.

In the final analysis, Johnny Cash isn't so far out of the blues trajectory. He grew up in the cotton fields in the little town of Dyess on the Arkansas side of the Mississippi Delta. In 1954, he found himself in Memphis outside Sam Phillips's Sun Studios on Union Avenue, just blocks away from the blues bars on Beale Street, where he recorded some of the best blues songs of the second half of the twentieth century, such as "Folsom Prison Blues" and "Cry, Cry, Cry." He's only seemingly out of place in a blues discussion. Not the least reason is that he wore black, or more accurately, because of the reason that he gave—in a song, of course. "Ah, I'd love to wear a rainbow every day/And tell the world that everything's OK," he sang, before adding, "But I'll try to carry off a little darkness on my back/Till things are brighter, I'm the Man in Black." As Steve Turner records in his biography, Cash was then asked if he was turning into a "political liberal." "No," Cash replied, "I'm just trying to be a good Christian." For Cash, too many were left out, too many left behind. He wrote the song "Man in Black" in 1971, with the backdrop of the Vietnam War giving meaning to his line mentioning a hundred dead bodies returning home every week. As long as those on the margins were still in need of a voice, Johnny Cash would wear black—not because he had rejected hope and life in favor of the dark side, but because he realized that grace triumphs in the harshness of life and sin.[18]

You can't get Johnny Cash without religion. Neither can you get the blues without religion. But is the reverse true? Can you get religion without the blues? To say that you can't is likely not totally true, but it may be partially so. It's worth considering the question. And it is the question taken up in the following chapters, which explore a theology in a minor key, a theomusicology of the blues. In broad strokes, a theology in a minor key embraces what we so often go to extremes to try to avoid in the contemporary world, the harshness and frailty of life, the presence of sin and evil, the shortcomings and limitations of humanity. In short, all of the realities of life under the curse. Blues invites us to embrace the curse through its articulation of restlessness and despair, longing and disappointment, exile and estrangement—what theologians call alienation. But a theology in a minor key also sounds a note of hope, as it leads us to the Man of Sorrows and the cross. The blues artists sang out of frustration, even vengeance.

The blues artists, however, *sang*, giving voice to their hope for deliverance, their hope that Sunday's coming. The blues invites us not only to embrace the curse but also simultaneously to embrace the cross. To see the broken made whole, the lost found. We see the exile and stranger make their way back home. "I was blind, but now I see," says the classic hymn. Not through some cheap happy ending, but in the identification and the defeat of all sorrow and sin in the Man of Sorrows on the cross, the most solemn minor key ever sounded in human history. In short, the blues helps us understand what theologians call redemption, all of the realities of life under the cross. The following chapters develop this further, harmonizing the blues with the rhythms of scripture and theology. For now, however, we can put the matter directly, returning to some lyrics cited earlier: "They call it stormy Monday," but, "Sunday I go to church, where I kneel down to pray. Lord have mercy, Lord have mercy on me."

«The Blues Highway», Highway 61, heading north just before Rolling Fork, Mississippi.

2

I Be's Troubled

Blues, the Bible, and the Human Condition

The blues were conceived in aching hearts.

W. C. Handy

I t was no Garden of Eden, no paradise. Life was difficult and cruel. Fruit didn't fall off trees. Instead, the fruit of this delta, cotton, had to be painstakingly picked by hand. About the only parallel between the Mississippi Delta and the Garden of Eden is that each had a river running through it. Nevertheless, there are parallels between bluesman Muddy Waters leaving the Delta and Adam and Eve getting expelled from the garden. Muddy Waters headed north first, then, like Adam and Eve, headed east. Just before he left, he recorded a song for Alan Lomax, as John Work stood by: "I Be's Troubled." Work titled it "I've Never Been Satisfied" in his field notes. It was later titled "I Can't be Satisfied," when it was recorded commercially at Chicago's Chess Records in 1948. The interaction between Work and Waters was also caught on tape:

> Work: How did you come to develop that one? Where did you first hear it?
>
> Waters: I made it up my own self. That's a song I made up.
>
> Work: How did you make it up? Tell us the story.
>
> Waters: The reason I come to make that record up once, I was just walking along the road, I heard a church song, kind of mind of that, I just dealed off a little song from that. And I started playing it.

The little song he "dealed off" went:

> Well, if I feel like tomorrow, like I feel today
> I'm gonna pack my suitcase, and make my getaway.
> I be troubled, I'm all worried in mind,
> And I never be satisfied, And I just can't keep from cryin'.

The last line he took from Blind Willie Johnson's 1928 Columbia recording, "Lord, I Just Can't Keep from Cryin' Sometime." From whom Blind Willie Johnson took the line is anybody's guess. The rest of the song Muddy Waters took from Adam and Eve and Genesis 3. The true parallel is that Muddy Waters and Adam and Eve were rolling stones.[1]

In "I Be's Troubled," Waters displays his restlessness and rootless wanderings. He takes both to new heights in a song he records in Chicago in 1950, "Rollin' Stone." Yes, this is the source of the name of rock's megaband. Keith Richards once said, "[Waters] named us, and we basically wanted to turn the world on to Muddy and his like. . . . I always thought that Muddy ran the band."[2] Muddy Waters's song is also the origin of Bob Dylan's song "Like a Rolling Stone" on his 1965 album *Highway 61 Revisited*. In the 1960s, the mostly white suburbanite youth audiences of Dylan, as well as of Mick Jagger, Keith Richards, and company, readily identified with what they took to be a cry of rebellious independence and shiftlessness, romanticizing the notion of a rolling stone just making its own way. What was lost on most of these middle-class audiences was that Muddy Waters, the root and source of all of this yearning, was not celebrating his independent, rambling life. He was mourning it.[3]

In taking his cue from Adam and Eve, Muddy Waters is in good company. Far from the cotton fields of Mississippi, among the cobblestone streets and ivoried gothic architecture of Cambridge, John Milton also took lines from Genesis 3, for his epochal *Paradise Lost*. Milton's Adam laments:

> O miserable of happy! Is this the end
> Of this new glorious World, and me so late
> The glory of that glory, who now, become
> Accursed of blessed.

"What can I increase," he asks, "Or multiply but curses on my head?" The coming generations, Milton's Adam muses prophetically, will reap the curse, and "for this," Adam can hear them saying, "we will have Adam to thank." Muddy Waters didn't read Milton, but he didn't have to in order to know the full force of Milton's verse. What Adam and Eve experienced, and John Milton and Muddy Waters gave poetic voice to, is the fallen state of the human condition, life under the curse. We be's troubled, and nothing can satisfy. This chapter explores this broken melody in both the Bible and the blues. We might prefer not to hear this broken melody. Our culture tends to celebrate achievements and triumphs, not failings and limitations. The blues and the Bible, however, force us to listen more deeply and honestly. The blues may very well be some of the most profoundly theological music, because it tells the truth.[4]

Of Rolling Stones and Hellhounds

Muddy Water spoke of wandering aimlessly, like a rolling stone. Robert Johnson put it a little more perniciously, speaking of being chased by a hellhound. More myth surrounds Robert Johnson than any other blues artist, perhaps even all the blues artists together. He made a deal with the devil, and he died on all fours howling like a dog, like the hellhound he so often sang of—at least, according to one of the legends. Or did he die, as his mother claimed, humming church songs, repentant and ready to meet his savior? Another legend claims he died by gunshot wound. As yet another story has it, he died by a stabbing. Or he was poisoned, presumably by the outraged husband of one of his dalliances—or, was it the father of one of his younger lovers? Someone had to put the poison in his whiskey, or stab him, or shoot him. Plenty of people had motive. His death certificate doesn't solve the mystery. "No Doctor" are the only words scrawled in the space provided for the cause of death. Not only are there different stories surrounding his death, but Robert Johnson is rumored to be buried in four different places. Three of the potential burial sites have markers for him, while John Hammond has proposed a fourth, yet unmarked, site.[5]

The mystery surrounding Johnson's life equals the mystery surrounding his death. Robert Santelli has said, "if Robert Johnson had never been born, the blues might have seen fit to invent him." He was born on May 8, 1911. And he died, at just twenty-seven years of age, on August 16, 1938. In between is legend, verging on myth.[6]

Johnson was born outside of the Delta in Hazlehurst, Mississippi, south of Jackson. He was the illegitimate son of Noah Johnson and Julia Major Dodds. During his childhood, Johnson passed from his mother to his mother's husband, then back to his mother and her new husband, not Johnson's natural father, settling in for the sharecropper's life on the

"Adam's Blues"

I was livin' in the desert, tryin' to get water from a
    stone.
I was livin' in the desert, tryin' to get water from a
    stone.
I got no place to go; I got no place to call my
    home.

                                                    SJN

Abbay & Leatherman plantation in Robinsonville. Now the
town is known for its own modest casinos standing in the
shadows of Tunica. In the 1920s and '30s the town, just a mile
or two east of the Mississippi and twenty or so miles south of
Memphis, consisted of the plantation Robert Johnson worked,
the Kirby-Wills plantation, and Foster's cafe, a juke joint that
regularly saw the likes of Charley Patton, Willie Brown, Son
House, and Louise Johnson.

Robert Johnson's schoolmates recall that he was quite good
on the harmonica and the Jew's harp. The instrument that
captured his attention the most, however, was the guitar.
Years later, Son House liked to recall his interaction with the
young, aspiring Robert Johnson, "He used to play harmonica
when he was 'round about fifteen, sixteen years old. He could
blow harmonica pretty good. Everybody liked it. But he just
got the idea that he wanted to play guitar."[7]

Going straight to a guitar was a bit out of reach for Johnson,
so he started on the "diddley bow," a creative but crude home-
made guitar that needed some nails, wire, and the side of a
house. This instrument, quite popular in the Depression-era

Delta, was made by hammering those nails into the side of a house and attaching a wire or two. A broken bottleneck served as the slide. Once a little money was saved up, guitars, such as they were, replaced the diddley bows. The bottleneck remained, producing that haunting slide sound of the early Delta blues.

Johnson imitated that sound, learned as he listened to Son House and Willie Brown, both of whom had somewhat settled in Robinsonville. Howlin' Wolf, born Chester Arthur Burnett, also played regularly in and around Robinsonville, since he worked on a nearby plantation. Throw into this mix the extensive time Charley Patton, hailed as the king of the Delta blues, spent playing in Robinsonville. Locals attributed this musical mecca to "lots of corn whiskey cooked up in these parts." Whatever drew these musicians there, one thing is certain, Johnson couldn't have been in a better place to come of age musically.[8]

But Robinsonville also gave Johnson plenty of heartache. Sometime before 1930, he married. Both his wife and his first child died in childbirth. And so Robert Johnson wandered. Reeling from his loss, he set out to find his natural father, Noah Johnson, whom he believed to be living back in Hazlehurst. While there's no evidence that he found him, he did find two things. First, he found the music of Tommy Johnson (no relation), who at this time was playing around Jackson. This Johnson would be somewhat of a protégé for the other one. Tommy Johnson recorded only a dozen songs, but his legend is as large as any of the blues musicians'. His music is marked by eerily screeched vocals and guitar riffs. And he fostered his reputation as one who had made a deal with the devil for his talent. All these attributes would find expression in the life and music of Robert Johnson.

During this time, Robert Johnson also found Callie Craft, whom he married. This second marriage was not blissful. Johnson took to the road, and whiskey and women followed. These were the beginnings of Robert Johnson's meteoric musical career, spanning the short time from around 1932 until his death in 1938.

What struck those who knew him best was his restlessness, his penchant for moving on—sometimes even in the middle of playing a set. As Johnnie Shines, who toured with Johnson, recalled, "Robert would just pick up and walk off and leave you standing there playing. And you wouldn't see Robert no more maybe in two or three weeks." Shines adds that "he was kind of long-armed," explaining, "What I mean by that, he'd kind of keep you away from him." As Johnson sang in "Hellhound on My Trail," "I've got to keep moving/ Blues falling down like hail/And the days keep on worrying me/There's a hellhound on my trail."[9]

In 1934 Johnson's travels with Johnnie Shines took him as far north as Canada, where they played some gospel music for *The Elder Moten Hour*. The partnership soon faded, and Johnson traveled and performed mostly by himself thereafter. Johnson finally received the invitation to record in 1936; in November, in a hotel in San Antonio, Texas, he recorded sixteen sides on the ARC label. A return trip in June 1937 would yield thirteen more recordings. In keeping with the practice of the day, Johnson was paid a flat fee for his music. He, like most of these blues musicians, never saw any royalties. He left both recording sessions with about $75 in his pocket, enough to pay for that snappy pin-striped suit he wears in a popular photograph of him. Although Johnson's songs met with modest success, he would never return to the studio. After playing in Greenwood one hot Saturday night, Johnson took terribly ill; it is believed he drank poisoned whiskey. He died a few days later, on August 16, 1938.

On one level, Johnson's life could be reduced to a morality tale: the stuff of melodramas, complete with youth and talent and vitality, all stripped away by too much drink and wild living. Admittedly, he's no role model. But reducing him to a mere warning sign seems shallow, even wrong. The trick to getting Johnson is listening to those twenty-nine recordings he left behind. As poet Alfred Encarnacion muses on Johnson:

> You sing a hard blues,
> black man. You too have been driven:
> a tumbleweed in strong wind.
> I close my eyes, your voice rolls
> out of the delta, sliding
> over flashy chords
> that clang like railroad tracks.[10]

"And Sin Was the Cause of It All"

The hard blues that Robert Johnson sang returned incessantly to three themes: women, ramblin', and the devil. If he was singing about cars ("Terraplane Blues") or even of dead shrimp ("Dead Shrimp Blues"), he was actually singing about women. Sometimes when he sang of women, he remembered his first wife, singing of her loss as well as the loss of his child. In "Preaching Blues" he painfully recalled, "Blues grabbed mama's child; and it tore me all upside down." But mostly he sang of women who have done him wrong. At one point he wished to have "possession over judgment day," so that these women who had wronged him would get their due. All these women troubles led him to ramble. "Walkin' Blues," which Johnson learned from Son House and which found its way into Muddy Waters's recordings, has him waking up looking for his shoes. He's been mistreated and so it's time to move on. In "Ramblin' on My Mind," Johnson's on the run once again because of a woman. His restless spirit caused him at one point to long for Chicago, or even faraway California, a place he could only dream of, in "Sweet Home Chicago." Johnson even expected to ramble in the life to come, pleading, "You may bury my body down by the highway side/So my old evil spirit can get a Greyhound bus and ride."[11]

46

And then there's that third theme, the devil, resounding in songs like "Me and the Devil Blues." Robert Johnson had learned from Tommy Johnson (who had learned it from someone else) of the power of the legendary musician who traded his soul for his talent. The idea is to meet the devil at the crossroads, around midnight, with guitar in hand. This devilish tradition even received attention in the Coen brothers' ironically delightful look at the darker side of pre–World War II Southern culture in *O Brother, Where Art Thou?* The tradition stretches back to African mythology. Legba, a sort of trickster deity, held sway over the crossroads, that literal and metaphorical point at which travelers and ramblers eventually arrive. As the slaves mingled their African folk religions with Christianity, Legba was replaced by the devil. And as the slaves, and their descendants, adapted their religious impulses to their new geographical environments, African crossroads were exchanged for the out-of-the-way crossings of back roads in the Delta.[12]

Robert Johnson appropriated the myth. And as he did, he was helped along by some apparent facts. First and foremost, he left Robinsonville unable to play the guitar, screeching out irritatingly shrill sounds as he grabbed up the guitar of Son House or of Willie Brown between sets. His playing was so bad that audiences pleaded for House and Brown to take their guitars with them when they stepped outside to get some air. Then Johnson suddenly returned to Robinsonville having mastered the instrument. No less than Eric Clapton testifies: "It is the finest music I have ever heard. I have always trusted its purity. I always will." Of course, two years intervened between his departure and celebrated return, plenty of time to learn to play. Son House liked to tell people it was less than six months, making the legend, the myth, a powerful tool. Johnson likely started the legend himself. Once the reputation took, he made sure to nurture it. Reputations are funny things. You make them, and then they make you.[13]

Three of his recorded songs helped further the reputation: "Cross Road Blues," "Hellhound on My Trail," and "Me and the Devil Blues." Elijah Wald has argued, in his attempt to deconstruct the myth of Johnson's transaction, that Robert Johnson "was working within a well-established tradition of blues devil songs." This tradition included the popular recordings of Peetie Wheatstraw, who liked to call himself the devil's son-in-law, and of Clara Smith's 1924 hit "Done Sold My Soul to the Devil." Wald even goes so far as to have an imaginary conversation between Johnson and the producer at the second recording session in June of 1937. That Peetie Wheatstraw stuff sells, the producer tells Johnson, adding, "How about some devil stuff?" Wald, on the one hand, may be congratulated for correcting the overinterpretation of the devil mythology in Johnson. On the other hand, Wald may have gone too far in underinterpreting these songs.[14]

In "Hellhound on My Trail," Johnson feels chased by something, something he fears. The line "blues falling down like hail" parallels "there's a hellhound on my trail." Framing this "dark night of the soul" in language that evokes Satan reveals the extent to which Johnson understood the sway Satan holds over this world. Johnson also knew the extent to which Satan held sway over his own life. Johnson has the blues in "Me and the Devil Blues" because of the things Johnson does when he's "walking side by side" with the devil, things that include beating his woman in the futile attempt to get some satisfaction out of it, playing to some primitive impulse. It's that old evil spirit who causes his own spirit to be so evil. Johnson wrestles with the flesh in most of his blues, but at times he wrestles with the dark angels, too. Most times, against both foes, he loses.

One of Johnson's most challenging songs to interpret is "Cross Road Blues." Legend has it that the crossroads that Johnson spoke of may be found just outside of Clarksdale, where both Highway 61 and Highway 49, meandering their respective ways north as escape routes from the Delta, cross paths. Tourists can have their picture taken under the oversized guitar suspended at the spot. Johnson's own "crossroads" likely had no such place in mind. The song evokes a much more remote location, more back roads than major highway. The curious thing about the song, however, is that it makes no reference to the devil. Johnson is at a crossroads, to be sure. But he appeals to God, not to the devil. As Johnson tells it, though, his plea to God falls unanswered. "Asked the Lord above have mercy: save poor Bob if you please," is met with a deadly silence. This leaves Johnson, by the end of the song, lamenting, "I believe I'm sinking down." Johnson had long since left the church. His mother tried to redeem him in memory by telling all who would listen that he spent his final days, dying from that poisoned whiskey, repentant and readying his soul for heaven. Taking this particular song as it stands, as well as what is known of Johnson's life, points in a different direction. Johnson's wanderings, from his marriage and around the Delta and beyond, can all be chalked up to his restless spirit, his sense of dereliction from God. Johnson sang of the devil because he felt abandoned by God.[15]

Robert Johnson, sounding much like the signature song of Muddy Waters, would cry out, "A Man is like a prisoner: and he's never satisfied." Even when Johnson tries to do right, he can only conclude that all of his "love's in vain." He couldn't seem to get past those "stones in his passway." "I have pains in my heart," he continues in this song, "they have taken my appetite." These insights into the human condition come to a climax in Johnson's admission in "Drunken Hearted Man." He's been "dogged," and he's been "driven" ever since he "left [his] mother's home"—ever since, in other words, he became a man. He's been dogged by "no-goods womens." His father died and left him, his mother "done the best that she could." But there's always whiskey, so he becomes the "drunken hearted man." He ends his "Preachin' Blues" with the same solution:

> Well the blues is a aching old heart disease
> Like consumption killing me by degrees
> Now if it's a starting a-raining I'm going to drive my
>   blues away
> Going to the stillery stay out there all day.

Yet even in this song, and especially in "Drunken Hearted Man," Johnson doesn't lie to himself when it comes to whiskey's limitations in redemption. The blues, like consumption, the old name for tuberculosis, is killing him. It's a heart disease. As he says it directly in "Drunken Hearted Man": "I'm a poor drunken-hearted man: and sin was the cause of it all." Not sins, but sin. The apostle Paul would agree.

Johnson gives voice to the root cause of this misery, this aching pain, this restlessness, this womanizing and carousing, this being chased by the hellhound, this existence that passed for his life. When Johnson identified sin as the cause, he likely had his own sin in mind. He also, knowingly or unknowingly, stumbled upon a more profound truth, the truth that Milton laid out in verse centuries earlier, the truth that Paul teaches is fundamental to the human condition, to all of those who are "in Adam," sons and daughters of the curse. That Johnson saw this is remarkable; that he saw himself beyond the pale of redemption is tragic.

It is also true that Johnson added to the sin of Adam, so to speak, heaping upon the curse more trouble, more sorrow, more pains of the heart. Apparently Robert Johnson didn't think Delta life had enough troubles, so he lived in such a way as to heap up more. Adam and Eve had enough troubles with thorns and serpents. Then Cain killed Abel. The curse, Milton mused, begets more curse. Sadly, Milton tends to be right. Johnson sang well, too well, of paradise lost.

"You Can't Lose What You Ain't Never Had"

Another Adamic type is Johnson's fellow Delta bluesman Muddy Waters. Born McKinley Morganfield in Issaquena County, in the southern Mississippi Delta, the musician who came to be known as Muddy Waters was raised by his grandmother after his mother's death. He had two recording sessions deep in the Delta while the world was at war. Once he heard himself, he knew he had a chance at heading north. He had once ventured to St. Louis but, perhaps not finding any hints of success, returned to the Delta. Those 78 recordings may have boosted his confidence enough, for he left the Stovall plantation and the sharecropper's life for good. He found himself on the crowded streets of Chicago, one of the major stopping points of the great northern migration of this era. Muddy's first recording sessions for Chess (at that time releasing under the label Aristocrat), cut in 1947, would be shelved for months. As Nadine Cahodas, in her story of Chess records, tells it, "Leonard [Chess] didn't get it. He was mystified, even irritated by Waters's indecipherable drawl." Apparently, Leonard's business partner at the time, Evelyn Aron, did get Muddy Waters. She pressed for more. In 1948 Waters returned to the Chess studio, recording "I Can't Be Satisfied," a reworking of a song he recorded for Alan Lomax back on the Stovall plantation in 1941. Back at Stovall, Waters titled the song "I Be's Troubled." Ironically, the 1948 recording lifted Waters from his troubles; the entire stock of the 78 sold out on the first day of its release to the public. Demand for it led to some price gouging. Waters himself was forced to buy a copy at $1.10, a full 31 cents above retail. After that it came near-constant touring, albums, Grammy Awards—including a lifetime achievement award given posthumously in 1992—international tours, and stardom. He even played at the White House for Jimmy Carter. Muddy Waters pulled off a rare feat, achieving both commercial and critical success, finding favor among musical purists at blues and folk festivals and among chain-store record buyers. Leonard Chess eventually got Waters. The two became quite close, with Waters confessing, "I tell everyone who asks that the one person responsible for my success is Leonard." Chess's fortunes rose alongside of Muddy Waters's. A lot of people besides Leonard Chess were getting exactly what Muddy Waters was up to, and they couldn't get enough.[16]

Muddy Waters is the bridge from prewar Delta blues to postwar rock 'n' roll. But—and here may be the secret to retaining his critical acclaim while racking up sales—his music is all Delta blues. In the lyrics, that is.

Like Robert Johnson, Muddy Waters liked to sing about women and whiskey. Unlike with Robert Johnson, the devil does not get his due. Muddy Waters could stockpile enough troubles on his own without the assistance of Satan. Something, nevertheless, did seem to empower Waters. Bravado, machismo, pounds through his music. "I'm Ready—as ready's anybody can be." "I'm a Man . . . No B-O—child—Y." No, he's all man. And, of course, he's "got his Mojo working," the closest he'll ever come to the darker side of the supernatural. All of this culminates in his declaration for the whole world: "I'm a Hoochie Coochie Man," complete with a shot across the bow, "Don't you mess with me." Such machismo, rife as it was with double entendres (this was the sixties), lends itself to the sign of his ultimate success: his music drafted in the service of a Viagra commercial.

But that's not quite the whole story of the music of Muddy Waters. Beneath the bravado lurks a great deal of uncertainty, unease, even sadness. While geographically he may have wandered far from the Stovall plantation, musically he stayed close to that 1941 recording of "I Be's Troubled." His was a troubled soul, having a hard time just trying to keep from crying. As with Robert Johnson, most of the time women were to blame. "Have you ever been mistreated?" he asks anyone who will listen. "She had the nerve to run me out," and this after he "work[ed] five long years for [her]." But it's not all the women's fault. The most famous lyric of his music, which was also a song title, and which may arguably be one of the most famous lyrics of all of rock 'n' roll, is his self-description as a "rolling stone." He doesn't come out and say that sin was the cause of it all, but it's there in between the lines.[17]

This restlessness and wandering left Muddy Waters with nowhere to go. He had moved up north and taken Chicago by storm. "I had Chicago sewed up in my hand," he once said. But, as he sings, "It's so cold up North that a bird can hardly fly." He'd not had love, and, the song tells us, he "ain't got no friend." Despite success, he still wasn't satisfied. He found it so cold—metaphorically—that he wanted to go back down south. But he couldn't. Waters sang, on another occasion, "Home is in the Delta" that he would soon be "leaving Chicago" to get back to it.[18]

That was, however, just a song. In real life he couldn't go back, and in fact he never did, except for concerts and blues festivals. Langston Hughes's character Roy Williams, from his story "Home," in *The Ways of White Folks*, also tried to go home, back to the South. Roy was a musician. He started out with blues and jazz. Then he headed north and became classically trained on the violin. A concert violinist, Roy was at home in the cities of the eastern seaboard and in Europe. Roy, we come to learn, may have been dying from tuberculosis, "the cough" that first hit him in Europe. And so he returned to his mother, to his home. He played for the children at the school, Brahms, Beethoven, such songs and such music as they had never heard. A few evenings later, Roy met the white schoolteacher on the streets. For his talking to her on the street, a black man talking to a white woman, Roy was beaten to death at the hands of an angry young white mob. Muddy Waters left the Delta for a reason. He wasn't going back. "They Call Me Muddy Waters," he sang in the 1971 hit, "I'm just as restless man as the deep blue sea."[19]

Muddy Waters was diagnosed with lung cancer in the spring of 1982. He began treatments but soon stopped.

Muddy's wife, Marva, whom he married in 1979, told the press, "He had made peace with the Lord and all he wanted was to be home with his family." He seemed to be getting along well, but by the next spring he had taken a downward turn. He was pronounced dead in a hospital in Downers Grove, a Chicago suburb, on April 30, 1983. He had died of a heart attack brought on by his cancer. Muddy Waters once said, "The blues was around way before I was born. They'll always be around. Long as people hurt, they'll be around."[20]

By this definition, Waters was well suited to sing the blues. Waters could sing of not having "a shelter over your head" in "Lonesome Road Blues, of "a hard, hard journey" in "One More Mile," and of "standing around crying" in the song by the same title. And he could reach all new depths of expressing loss when he insightfully mused, "You can't lose what you ain't never had." Waters, like Robert Johnson before him, toyed with looking for redemption. Mostly, he looked in the direction of whiskey for it. "If the river was whiskey," adding another condition, "and I was a divin' duck," then, he concluded, he would simply "dive to the bottom" and would never come back up. But at the end of "Rollin' and Tumblin,'" he took this carefree lyric in a haunting direction. Waters tells us that he "could a had a religion," but all that whiskey and women—and here he took lines straight from Furry Lewis and Son House—"would not let him pray." Waters, once again like Robert Johnson before him, didn't pray. Jon Michael Spencer explains why: "It was orthodox 'blues belief' that those who chose to sing the blues were gambling away their chance to reap the eternal bounty and would reap what they sowed."[21]

Maybe at the end, as his wife, Marva, told the press, Waters had found peace with God. In his songs, though, that peace eludes him. Earlier in his life Waters did call out to God. In "I Be's Troubled," he pleads, "Lord I'm troubled, I'm all worried in my mind." Again Spencer sets this in context for us by arguing that "the 'oh Lord' interpolation in the blues was not a theologically meaningless apostrophe." Crying out to the Lord wasn't simply put in for effect, or some type of musical filler. It had meaning. In Muddy Waters's case, as with nearly all the blues artists, crying out to the Lord was something he had learned in his grandmother's church. A faithful churchgoing Baptist, she saw to it that while Muddy was young he would be in church, even holding out hope that he would someday be a pastor. As he grew and turned to music, his Saturday nights lasted so long, his Sunday mornings were not spent in church. Muddy recalled a conversation he had with his grandmother, "She say I couldn't be playing. I should go to church. Finally, I say I'm doing this, I'm goin' to do it. And she got where she didn't bother me about it." His whiskey and his women wouldn't let him pray. But, his songs reveal that what he learned in that Baptist church never left him at all.[22]

Embracing the Curse

The human condition, as Friedrich Nietzsche spoke of it, is frail and weak, and must be overcome. No God will help, he further argued. We must look to ourselves, finding the strength to overcome from within, to become the *ubermensch*. Alas, Nietzsche died insane and ravaged by syphilis. His thought, however, lives on. Shunned in his day, Nietzsche became the darling of post–World War II French existentialists, blues artists working in a different language and a different medium. They, like Nietzsche, saw the despair and meaninglessness of life. They too had a prescription. For Sartre and Camus the answer to the human condition was simply to act, to choose. And in that action and in that choice we become, we make ourselves, we *exist*. The problem with Nietzsche and Sartre and Camus is that they are half-wrong. Of course, that means they are also half-right. And the half-right part is worth paying attention to. That half-right part has to do with the limitations, frailty, and weakness that define the human condition. Sin, Robert Johnson reminds us, was the cause of it all.

And so we are led back to the original blues song, a duet, sung by Adam and Eve. We are baffled imagining the world they inhabited before the fall. A world of shalom and harmony. But that peace was fractured as sin entered the garden. None but Adam and Eve know the true depth and weight of the loss. We are left only to imagine that world they inhabited, the pre-fallen world in which they lived and worked. They were punctured by the greatest of losses. But we do know the new world they entered once they were banished from the garden, the world under the curse. The Genesis account tells us that the curse would be the new norm for life outside the garden. From then on, the world, Dietrich Bonhoeffer laments, "drops blindly into infinite space, like a meteor that has torn itself away from the core to which it once belonged. It is of this fallen-falling world that we must now speak."[23]

Adam and Eve reluctantly embraced the curse. Bonhoeffer, in addition to likening the fall to a meteor, also spoke of the fall as limit, a limit that "assails Adam . . . Adam keeps on running up against it; it is always in the way." Adam and Eve learned to live in the new world, this world of limit. When they went out from the garden as exiles, they settled to the east of Eden. In keeping with the command to have dominion over the earth and to subdue it, they worked, and, in keeping with the command to increase, they gave birth to at least two sons, Cain and Abel. Abel, too, embraced his new role, serving God as he could. But Cain rebelled against the curse itself, against the limit. God would not accept him, and Cain would not accept such a limitation. Cain acted by taking the curse to new depths, as brother turned on brother. And Lamech, Cain's descendant, took the curse even deeper still. Adam and Eve respond to all of this by having another son, Seth, whose name means "granted." Seth was a gift from God in the place of the loss of Abel, a little grace in a cursed world.[24]

If anyone knew the pain of loss, the depth to which the human heart can sink and the literal carnage left in its wake, it was Adam and Eve. When Paul speaks of the wretched person in Romans, he could speak of his self; but the original wretched man was Adam, and the original wretched woman was Eve. There is no record of how they responded to all this loss and disruption of shalom, beyond their bickering in Genesis 3:11–13. In them, however, can be seen the two themes that will dominate life under the curse, the themes of exile and exodus. These were the first exiles, forced to abandon their home in the garden and to seek out a new place. There had been no outsiders in the garden. Now, ironically, there would be no insiders. All humanity would bear the status "exile"; all of us are wanderers.

There are many words used to convey the notion and concept of sin in the Bible. Many of them are picturesque, perhaps none more so than the Greek word *planao*, which means "to wander." The English word *planet* derives from this word. Ancient Greek astronomers referred to these celestial bodies that they observed as wanderers about the sky. To sin is to wander, to be restless and rootless, homeless. Lost sheep. It's Israel in the desert, out of the harsh but familiar surroundings of Egypt and far away from the Promised Land. In our present-day culture of mobility, in terms of geography, vocation, and relationships, such *planao*, such wandering, is hardly taken as tragic. Rather, it's simply seen as the norm, as the way things are. On occasion, however, such wandering can be seen for what it truly is. This wandering is understood as, borrowing a phrase from Cornelius Plantinga, Jr., not the way it's supposed to be.[25] It leaves a nagging realization that all of this wandering isn't right. It's an aching old heart disease called the blues.

A lot of people talk about getting in touch with their roots. Very few actually do so. Had Adam and Eve tried to get in touch with their roots, they would have been met with an angelic being, sword "whirling and flashing" (Gen. 3:24 REB). Their hope to eventually return to the place of blessing, the place of shalom, lay outside of themselves and in the promised seed of blessing who would overcome the curse. It wasn't Abel, it wasn't Seth. Neither was it any from that long list of descendants ticked off in Genesis 5. It wasn't even Noah, neither was it Abraham, and neither was it Joseph. Adam and Eve and all those to follow after them long for *exodus*, that second theme that pervades the biblical narrative. Exile points to our lostness, wandering, the condition of *planao*. Exodus points us home. It takes us from the east of Eden and puts us back in Eden. The one who would bring about this exodus would be the seed, the lace of promise amidst the flood of curse in Genesis 3. Remarkably, this seed himself would experience exile, even dereliction. As Luther said, and as Dietrich Bonhoeffer repeated for the twentieth century, Christ came into this world, and this world pushed him away, all the way on to the cross. And as he hung there, he was forsaken by God. "Oh Lord," he cried out, a fully theologically meaningful interpolation. In fact, his "Oh Lord" becomes the intensely intimate "My God, my God." He was met with silence. And darkness canopied the earth.

We want to rush on in the biblical story. We want to rush on in the story of our lives. We want Easter Sunday, when the sun rises and the morning returns the light. The blues makes us wait in darkness. Henry Townsend, a Delta bluesman who made his home in St. Louis, once said, attempting to justify his life and work, "If I sing the blues and tell the truth, what have I done?" The answer is that he has been a theologian, one who has spoken the truth of the human condition. This is the truth of the blues, first sung by Adam and Eve and then echoed throughout human history. This long, human song finds perhaps its most authentic expression in the music arising from the plantations of the Mississippi Delta.[26]

This present discussion has looked at the Adamic types of Robert Johnson and Muddy Waters, musicians who stumbled into theology. The next two chapters explore more examples of exile and exodus, more examples of embracing the curse and longing for redemption. Chapter 5 presents us with hope, hope sprung from a cross. Upon that cross, the Seed undid what Adam and Eve had done. Upon that cross, the Seed conquers the "sin [that] was the cause of it all."

Billups Plantation office and commissary,
off Highway 82, west of Indianola, Mississippi.

3

Man of Sorrows

David's Blues

I got a letter this morning, how do you reckon it
read?
It said, "Hurry, hurry, yeah, your love is dead."

"Dead Letter Blues," Son House

For when I kept silent, my bones wasted away
through my groaning all day long.

Psalm 32:3, a maskil of David

In his poem "Christmas Trees," Geoffrey Hill imagines
himself sitting beside Dietrich Bonhoeffer in his prison
cell. The first three lines lull us into sad reflection on the
German theologian's suffering and imprisonment. Then Hill
jars us in the very next line when he proclaims that Bonhoeffer "restores the broken themes of praise." From the depths

David would cry, and the Lord heard him. Have mercy, David begged. God listened, and David could sing his new song. Sometimes it would take a while; the wait must have seemed interminable. Often it would take more than three lines, and sometimes David would have to wail through his whole song, not finding any relief, any resolution, until the very end, until that last line. But eventually, the psalmist, a man of many sorrows, would be led to praise.

David was many things: a shepherd, a husband (a few times over), a father to a challenging band of siblings, a warrior, a friend. He is best known as a king. But before he was a king, he was a musician who played stringed instruments. I would argue, risking anachronism, that he was a blues musician. He sang of famine, war, death. According to 2 Samuel 21, he even faced giants—literal ones. "When the waves of death encompassed and destructive torrents overtook me," David moans in 2 Samuel 22, "I cried to the Lord . . . and my cry reached his ears." David could speak of stormy nights, thunder rolling. He could also speak of "the light of morning at sunrise." When he kept silent, his "bones wasted away" (Ps. 32:3). When he sang, when he gave voice to his miserable groaning, praise eventually broke out: "Be glad in the LORD and rejoice" (Ps. 32:11 NASB). Where did the melody of praise come from?

Genesis 3 has a lot of woe, curse, and misery. As we saw in the last chapter, it is the exile song. David knew this dark side of Genesis 3. He had been afflicted by the sin of Adam and had heaped his own sin upon the pile. He had taken life, and he had watched helplessly as lives he loved were taken (2 Sam. 12). But Genesis 3 also tells a tale of grace. It has that ray of promise, resting entirely in the seed of the woman. This is the hope of the Messiah, the seed to come who would deliver humanity from the curse of sin. As the pages of the biblical canon unfold, this promise of the seed becomes amplified. David knew of this seed. Some of his subjects even believed David to be the seed, the deliverer. David knew better, for he knew exactly what he was capable of and not capable of. At one point, David may have thought that his own son would be the seed. He may have believed, or at least hoped, that through Solomon, God would return his blessing to the children of Israel, delivering them from famines and wars and giants in the Promised Land, delivering them from reaping the full harvest of David's own sin. As the story unfolded before David's eyes, however, he began to realize that Solomon wasn't the seed, which was yet to come. The mere promise of the seed, however, was enough for David to have hope, enough to restore praise to his broken melodies and fractured world. The seed was the reason he could sing.

Both sides of Genesis 3, the darker side of the curse and the brighter side of the seed, gave David plenty from which to sing. David also knew the song of exile, the other theme in Genesis 3. David had been an outsider, he had been overlooked. His startling career as king began rather embarrassingly. The biblical text of 1 Samuel 16 recalls how Samuel had been sent to David's father's home to anoint the next king. Jesse, David's father, paraded his sons before the aging prophet. Samuel was nonplussed by all of them and asked Jesse if he had any more sons. Almost as an afterthought, Jesse remembered David, the youngest, who had been out tending sheep. At Samuel's pleading, Jesse fetched him and, absent any fanfare, Samuel anointed him king. The route from David's anointing to his enthronement was circuitous. In the prime of his life he was hunted like an animal in the wilderness of Judea and beyond. Chased by King Saul and his armies, it was David against the world. Furthermore, David lived riddled with guilt. From this hard life came his beautiful, sometimes haunting, music. While it may be anachronistic to call David a bluesman, he could, by the credentials born of his suffering and by the repertoire he left behind, rival any of the Mississippi Delta's finest. David and the blues artists certainly have shared experiences, despite being divided by centuries, oceans, and languages. They even have shared responses to those experiences. These were men and women of sorrows, who, as they sang their sorrow songs, longed for praise to break in. The pages below explore some of these singers and their songs.

Who's That Writin'?

An elderly man sits on a stool in front of an audience. You sense that you are in the presence of a legend, watching someone and something from a different era, a distant world. You sense that this man has something profound to give away, something born of a difficult life. With hardened hands and weathered face, he sits holding a guitar. He's not playing it, just using it to slap out a beat. "Tell me who's that writin'?" his gravelly voice asks, and he answers his own question, "John the Revelator." With more intensity he repeats it: "Tell me who's that writin'? / John the Revelator." For a third time, almost impatiently, he asks and answers, "Who's that writin'? /John the Revelator, wrote the book of the seven seals." You are left with the impression that there is nothing else quite like this. What's even more remarkable is that the man on the stool, Son House, was discovered by accident—not just once, but twice.

As we saw in chapter 1, Alan Lomax trekked into the Delta in 1941 on a mission to record an endangered music. He had hoped to find the legendary Robert Johnson. Lomax wanted to record Johnson, not in some hotel room with a record company's equipment, but in the field, on the porch of the juke joint, commissary, or cypress shack he called home. Lomax missed him by about three years. Instead he found Robert Johnson's musical father, Son House. When you remember that Lomax's other discovery was Muddy Waters, you realize that Alan Lomax couldn't have been too disappointed in his trip. For Son House, though, it was likely a bittersweet experience.

"Nehemiah's Blues"

When I heard this, I wept.
—Nehemiah 1:4

Let me weep,
Let me weep.

Let me weep,
Let me weep.
But let me pray.

SJN

Son House came to the blues later in his life. He was born Eddie James, Jr., on March 21, 1902, in the Delta town of Riverton, Mississippi. His youth was spent working the plantation fields during the week and sitting in the church pew on Sundays. Before reaching his twentieth birthday, he became a Baptist pastor. But his soul seemed restless. Eventually, he would split his weekends, continuing to devote his Sundays to church but giving his Saturdays to the juke joint. He even left the Delta for a time in the early 1920s. He came back and taught himself to play a guitar. A lot rested on that guitar. Son House saw it as his redemption. A story is told of a grateful fan visiting an aged Son House convalescing in his Detroit nursing home in the late 1980s. The fan brought along a National guitar. The eyes of a listless old man lit up at the mere sight of it and, impulsively, he reached for it. Son

House had started playing the guitar some six decades earlier, performing at house parties and juke joints in the Delta in the late 1920s. One public performance came to an abrupt end as one of the frequent fights—the local term for a juke joint was a "bucket of blood"—ended in Son House drawing his pistol and shooting a man to death. He was off to Parchman Prison. He served a year, a merciful judge releasing him after he reviewed his case and determined Son House's action to have been self-defense.[1]

House teamed up with Charley Patton, himself a Baptist pastor and blues musician, and Willie Brown. The three were invited to Grafton, Wisconsin, to record for Paramount. House recorded six sides, among them "Walking Blues," a song his musical protégé Robert Johnson would record a few years later. It speaks of that restlessness, rambling, and wandering that reverberates through the blues. He also recorded "Dry Spell Blues," which laments a drought in the South, "My Black Mama," "M&O Blues," and "Future Blues." The final song of these sessions became somewhat of a signature song for Son House; in "Preachin' Blues," with just a hint of sarcasm, House begins by telling us he's "gonna be a Baptist preacher" so he "won't have to work." In the second stanza he makes a reference to that other stage in his past, his time as a convict, a bit of a roadblock to his pastoral aspirations. The real culprit comes in the third stanza:

> Oh, I went in my room, I bowed down to pray
> Oh, I went in my room, I bowed down to pray
> Till the blues come along and they blowed my spirit
> away.

It wasn't all the fault of the blues. In the fourth stanza he turns to the old standbys, "womens and whiskey." They were just too much for him, "they would not set [him] free."

The question is how to interpret the "blues" that came along in the third stanza. Does Son House mean the music, the life, the juke joints, and the whiskey and women that were inside of those juke joints? Or does Son House mean something different by the blues? Does he mean, as he will come later to define the blues, "the worried old heart disease" that tugs at him, that human condition that plagues creatures and creation? If it's the latter, then that which kept him from praying wasn't the music after all. Instead, it was praying and not hearing any answers, especially answers to all the blues that were around him. In his last concert in the United Kingdom, at the 100 Club in London, Son House tells the audience, in between songs, that he's heard of the old blues singers who would plead, Lord have mercy, when it comes time to die. He said, "I don't want that. I wanted to have some of his mercy now." Son House looked for mercy, but apparently couldn't find it.

In one of those 1930 Paramount session songs, Son House makes an impassioned plea for mercy. There's a drought, "a dry old spell everywhere." So he "stood in his backyard, wrung [his] hands and screamed." He screamed a petition:

> Lord have mercy if you please
> Lord have mercy if you please
> Let your rain come down and give our poor hearts
> ease.

As the song rolls on, he pleads even more strenuously, exclaiming "these blues is worthwhile to be heard." It wasn't only droughts that sent him on his knees. In "Death Letter Blues," he was again in his room praying when the blues "came along and drove his spirit away." The blues this time was a letter, telling him the woman he loved was dead. And, again, he turned to the Lord for mercy. This time he adds, "Lord have mercy on my *wicked* soul." Was he somehow complicit? Had he fought with her, causing her to leave, to encounter trouble, and to end up on "the coolin' board"? Had he left her after a fight, leaving her vulnerable? His grief shows he loved her.

But maybe now he regrets something he had done. What we know for certain is that she's gone, and all he's left with is an emptiness she once filled. Son House's songs continually plead for mercy. Most times there's no answer. Son House wanted one. "The blues came and got you," he once sang.[2]

In "How to Treat a Man," Son House takes on the blues directly. "Go away blues," he commands them, "Go away and leave poor me alone." In this song, blues means more than the music. It's that aching old heart disease once again. David also pled for mercy on more than one occasion, and at times the blues seemed to be getting the upper hand. But then the broken melody of praise would break in. House let praise break in, too. He could reel off a string of blues and then follow it with a rendition of "This Little Light of Mine." Jesus gave it to him, he declared, now he's going to let this little light shine. He may have felt at times that his prayers for mercy went unanswered, but he still kept asking. "May the good Lord be with you," he would say in a hushed tone as he was about to step off the stage. As David Evans explains it, this is Son House, the preacher, pronouncing a benediction over his audience. It was his prayer, uttered in reverence and in faith.[3]

Son House may have had his share of difficulties, but he knew how the story would end. Perhaps, if there is such a thing, the singular moment in American music, that moment which is pure and authentic, came in Son House's "John the Revelator." The song takes the form of the holler songs, born out of the slave experience, matured in the days of Reconstruction sharecropping and, in the case of Son House, aged at places like Parchman. These were call-and-response songs, bringing about, in the words of Alan Lomax, "a healthy sense of community." The hollers were a way of getting by, of coping with inhumane experiences.[4]

Son House came by his slide guitar style the same way most blues musicians learned their trade, by imitation. The man who taught him, informally, was one of the lesser-known stars of the blues constellation, Rubin Lacy. That Lacy is not as well known as some of his fellow blues musicians may be because he produced only two sides, for Paramount in 1928. He had recorded four sides for Columbia, but they were never issued. Lacy let the church steal him away from the blues. Born in Pelahatchie, Mississippi, in 1901, Lacy became a major figure in the Jackson area and around the lower Delta. The church, as in the case of Son House, tugged at him. And as with Son House, that tug came from grandparents; Lacy's grandfather was a Baptist pastor. "Rube" felt the pull to the church too strong. By 1932, he left the blues and followed in his grandfather's footsteps.

While he was the itinerant bluesman, he recorded two songs, "Mississippi Jail House Groan" and "Ham Hound Crave." The first one has a lot of moaning in it, something he learned in church. He finds himself in jail, "back turned to the wall." His mother comes to visit but won't bring the jail house "key." She won't help him get out from under the charges; he would have to pay for his crime. "I looked at my mama," he groans as he is confronted with his plight, "and I hung my head and cried." In his next song, "Ham Hound Crave," a double entendre, Lacy also reveals something he learned in church. Tucked away in the middle of the song is a rather telling line: "The dirty deacon has taken my gal and gone." In 1927, one year before Lacy made this recording, Luke Jordan recorded "Church Bells Blues" for Victor. This song takes an even deeper swipe at hypocrisy in the church. Jordan indicts the church in the first lines:

> Children's in the pulpit, mama trying to learn the
> psalms
> Now the lowdown dirty deacon, done stole my gal
> and gone
> Woke up this morning, the family had the weary
> blues.

Deacons weren't the only ones running off with other men's wives. Preachers were also known to steal away a wife or two. Lacy eventually saw past the hypocrisy, turning to the ministry. He would still sing—just gospel. He was even known to break into song during his sermons. That he had rhythm didn't hurt his cadence for sermonizing. It was a bit of a two-way street: his blues infused his preaching and gospel singing, and his gospel singing, preaching, and church life infused his blues. The same was true for his protégé, Son House.[5]

The story has it that House would play the blues all through Saturday night and well into the predawn hours of Sunday morning. Roused by the sunrise and realizing that it happened to be Sunday, he would wake those sleeping off the whiskey. He would find someplace to stand, on the platform or on the bar or on a table, and would start preaching—presumably not against the evils of strong drink. After a bit of fire and brimstone, he would step down, find his guitar and play on and on until the crowd had to leave to get some sleep for work the next morning. As time progressed, the preaching stints in the midst of the blues weekend marathons tapered off, then disappeared altogether. Rarely, though, even when he was in that preaching mode, did he step into the church. The blues, that nagging human condition tearing away at his soul, and all that hypocrisy were just too much.

Another voice joined the team of Rubin Lacy and Son House, that of the legendary Charley Patton. If Robert Johnson holds the position of king of the Delta blues, that of founder may very well be attributed to Charley Patton. He too has that strange mix of women, whiskey, preaching, and singing the blues. Patton was born in 1891 (some contend it was 1881, while others put it at 1887) in Edwards, Mississippi, in between Vicksburg and Jackson. He came of musical age in the heart of the Delta on the Dockery plantation, nestled in between Highways 49 and 61. Patton learned to play the guitar by the age of seven, playing for house parties and making money by the age of ten, according to one of his nieces. While working the cotton fields with Dockery's 2,000 employees and working for his father, who ran some timber wagons, he perfected his playing during his teenage years. By the early 1920s, he was ready to leave the Dockery plantation. Those two highways on either side of him were just too tempting. Patton's guitar brought him freedom.[6]

During that decade Patton traveled throughout the Delta and beyond, traveling to play at lumber camps as far away as Georgia. Many of the blues musicians recorded in the 1920s were imitating him, playing his songs, using his guitar licks, and borrowing his lyrics. Those musicians very likely had heard him play and were to some degree inspired by him. Yet Charley Patton wouldn't have his own recording session until 1929, in Richmond, Indiana. Later recording sessions would take him to Grafton, Wisconsin—with Son House and Willie Brown—Chicago, and New York City. He recorded well over sixty songs, including blues, gospel, and folk ballads. His career ended on April 28, 1934, when he died of heart failure in Indianola, Mississippi, the same town that B. B. King calls home.

Charley Patton's repertoire is the blues. He sings about it all: the hard life, rambling, calamity, trouble with women, whiskey, run-ins with the law, and frequent pleas to the Lord. In "Down the Dirt Road Blues," he moans, "Every day seem like murder here, I'm going to leave tomorrow." He faced both natural calamities and those of his own making. He sang about the great Mississippi River flood in 1927, a historical event that recaptured attention in the aftermath of Hurricane Katrina's devastation. The 1927 flood became well memorialized in song. Bessie Smith's "Backwater Blues," Blind Lemon Jefferson's "Risin' High Water Blues," and Robert "Barbecue Bob" Hicks's "Mississippi Heavy Water Blues" were just some of the blues memorials. Charley Patton pays the flood tribute in "High Water Everywhere," from his first recordings in 1929. There were Mississippi River floods before this, especially before the levee system was built, and there would be floods after. Johnny Cash sings of the 1937 flood in "Five Feet High and Rising." But none of these floods took a toll as heavy as the great flood in 1927. The Army Corps of Engineers assured communities all along the river that the levees would hold, but they didn't. When the waters finally receded, over 26,000 square miles had been flooded, hundreds of lives were lost, and an estimated 600,000 people found themselves homeless and displaced. Most of those left for the North, triggering a wave of migration. Some places encountered twenty-foot depths of water. Blind Lemon Jefferson paints the picture in his blues:

> Thousand people stands on the hill, looking down
>   where they used to stay
> Children stand there screaming, mama we ain't got
>   no home
> Papa says to children, black water left us all alone.

"I leave," Jefferson closes his lament, "with a prayer in my heart." But some, as Bessie Smith's "Back Water Blues" has it, had nowhere to go:

> I can't move no more
> There ain't no place for an old girl to go.

Her blues doesn't end with a prayer. It just ends.[7]

In 1929, the Delta region experienced the other extreme, as drought ruined the crops for yet another year and seriously threatened the livelihood and very lives of the sharecroppers. Patton sings of this in "Dry Well Blues." Son House recorded a song by the same name. Both were living in the town of Lula, Mississippi, at the time. The dry weather, in Patton's song, had "parched all the cotton and corn," leaving him with no money and no home. His plea was simply "Lord, you ought to been there," Patton's desire for God to be sympathetic to his plight, to show mercy.

Alongside floods and drought another plague hit the Delta. A tiny insect had migrated from Mexico, through Texas, Louisiana, and Arkansas, on into the Delta and then beyond. It was the infamous boll weevil. In his study of cotton, Stephen Yafa notes the relationship between the rise of the Delta blues and the boll weevil: "The blues and boll weevil might have each existed in the absence of the other, but with nothing like the earthy profundity, depth of desperation, or resigned acceptance of fate that the ruinous pest bestowed on the music." It might be an overstatement to attribute the rise of the blues to the boll weevil, but the "ruinous pest" gave blues singers plenty of material. The female boll weevil would bore a hole in the bud of the cotton, called the square, where she would lay her eggs. Or she would leave her eggs, hundreds of them, on the seed pod or the "boll" of the cotton. Yafa explains the result: "As hatching larvae destroyed the tissue of squares or new bolls, the vegetation would fall off. Rows of dead squares littering the ground overnight became a common, dreaded sight." Neither Charley Patton nor the tens of thousands of sharecroppers across the Delta could defeat the boll weevil. All they could do was sing about it. "Boll weevil told the farmer that I ain't gonna treat you fair," Patton sang. "Took all the blossoms and leave you an empty square." He and the other sharecroppers and blues musicians had experience dealing with things beyond their control. Sometimes the blues singers seemed to champion the beetle, for the ones hurt most by it were the plantation owners. The insect, it seems, brought some sort of justice with it.[8]

Racial oppression certainly topped the list of experiences of those forces beyond control. Patton had more respect for the boll weevil than he did for white supremacists. David Evans has argued that Charley Patton resisted the status quo, the ever-present pressure to acquiesce, of the post–Reconstruction-era South. Patton's music and his life, Evans argues accordingly, were infused with a little rage. He may have resolved himself to the fate brought on by the boll weevil, but he had a little fight in him when it came to the question of race. Evans points out that Patton speaks disparagingly of white deputies and sheriffs in "Tom Rushen Blues." In this song, as well as in the similar "High Sheriff Blues," Patton names names: Tom Rushen and Tom Day, real people, real white people. Blues singers didn't flinch from castigating their white oppressors, but usually did so generically, as "boss man" or "captain." They used code. It was, as Evans notes, virtually unknown for a black man, one who would still travel the Delta, to criticize a white man by name, especially one who held an office of power. But Patton did.[9]

Charley Patton also gave himself plenty of material to work with through troubles of his own making. He once triggered the jealousy of a husband, resulting in Patton's throat getting cut. He nearly died, and he carried a severe scar as a reminder. Patton often wore a scarf to cover it up. Most times he would simply raise his collar on that side—it was said that from the mid-1920s on he always wore a suit. His only surviving photograph shows a raised right collar. Patton's family members claimed he had married eight times, not always divorcing. Court records have been found for six of the marriages; that they were in different counties allowed for the bigamy. He had multiple children with these wives, and some children with women beyond these eight. Some reports exist that he could be abusive in these relationships. As with the other bluesmen, both women and whiskey became his vices: "It take boozy booze, Lord, to carry me through," he confesses in "Tom Rushen Blues."

Neither the women nor the whiskey could keep him from singing gospel. Patton's family likely expected him to be a preacher. His father, Bill Patton, never cared much for his guitar, and a niece reported that his grandmother reluctantly succumbed to recognizing her grandson's career of singing and guitar playing. Yet, while never formally becoming a minister, Patton wouldn't be kept from preaching.

And, like his colleagues, Charley Patton also sang of the hypocrisy riddling the church. His "Elder Greene Blues" recalls the philandering churchman, much akin to that lowdown dirty deacon Son House and others sang of. Patton's song contains a bit of memoir. When he sings, "I love to fuss and fight, Lord, and get sloppy drunk off o' bottle," the first person is not likely just a reference to the fictional Elder Greene. Patton is Elder Greene, beset by his vices and forced to get away. The song, rather than celebrating this wild life on the run, functions like a confession. He's mourning his vices and the trouble they've caused, not celebrating them.

Charley Patton hoped such confession might lead to repentance and that such repentance might lead to redemption. If that repentance and redemption didn't come in this life, maybe it would come for him in the end. So he recorded, "You're Gonna Need Somebody When You Die," in which Patton breaks out in a sermon. The person he needed, the song reveals, is Jesus. Patton makes his plea even more explicit in "Jesus Is a Dying Bed Maker." He had one hope in life—that Jesus would make up his dying bed. "I got religion," he repeats three times, with each line growing louder and more intense. He's acting as his own lawyer, making his case.

Such singing of deathbed repentance became strangely prophetic. After experiencing some heart trouble, Patton paid a visit to a doctor, who told him the gravity of his condition. The doctor prescribed a time of convalescence to strengthen his weak heart, a prescription requiring Patton to put down the guitar that had been in his hands for decades. Patton ignored the advice, leaving for recording sessions in New York in January and February. But by April, having returned to the Delta, Patton sensed the end was coming. He lived in the back of the store in Holly Ridge, Mississippi.

Holly Ridge had a cotton gin, the New Jerusalem Missionary Baptist Church, one store, railroad tracks, rows of sharecropper shacks, and hundreds of acres of cotton. In Holly Ridge, Charley Patton finally put down his guitar. Instead of taking to his bed, however, he started preaching. His niece, Bessie Turner, recalls the last weeks of his life: "He started to preach that morning [Saturday April 21]. He preached all that week, and the next Saturday he passed on." Patton's favorite text was the Book of Revelation, picking out the themes of death, of the life to come, and of heaven. He also sang when he preached. The song he came back to again and again in those sermons preached as he clung to life in that last week, was a simple little chorus:

> Jesus is my God, I know his name.
> His name is all my trust.
> He would not put my soul to shame,
> Or let my hopes be lost.

Interpretations of the life and personality of Charley Patton range from viewing him as heroic to writing him off as a "degenerative sociopath." In between there are the sympathetic critics who excuse his foibles by attributing them to the customs of the day. Interpretations of his music also range widely, from considering it incoherent garbling to mere entertainment. He even developed the trick of quickly and deftly swinging his guitar around his back and continuing on playing without so much as missing a chord. He frequently modulated his voice to mimic his guitar, and used his guitar to mimic his voice. A case could be made that he was a showman. There's also a strong case to be made, however, that beneath all of that showmanship there lies some serious social criticism. As the founder of the blues, an often cryptic and mysterious musical form, it's fitting that he should be an enigma for us. His vices shouldn't be overlooked; his womanizing and bigamous ways can't be excused or brushed aside (I hope my in-laws see that I lodge this criticism.). There is something compelling about him and his music, however, that deserves notice.

William Ferris, in his slightly dated but still remarkably insightful study of the blues, explores the relationship between the church and the blues. He notes that while some called the blues the devil's music, "blues singers call on the Lord for support." Ferris continues, "Blues singers feel their music describes life as it is, with an honesty not found in the church." In these brief sketches of Son House and Charley Patton, both of these observations by Ferris boldly ring true. A number of things kept House from the church, including the hypocrisy in the church and House's own vices. But the tipping point was the harsh conditions that Delta folks had to live through without, from all that House could see, any divine help. These same issues barred Charley Patton. While they might have given up on the church, Son House and especially Charley Patton didn't give up on the Lord. And they both hoped and prayed that the Lord hadn't given up on them. They produced profound music that affected an entire art form, the Delta blues, which in turn affected American music throughout the twentieth century.[10]

Their music came from their lives. It flowed from their frustrations with weather, weevils, and women, from their sins, their confessions, and their hopes for redemption. It is Christ-haunted music, because it so honestly portrays life under the curse. It is beauty. W. E. B. Du Bois once described the music of this time and place as "that plaintive rhythmic melody, with its touching minor cadences, which, despite caricature and defilement, still remains the most original and beautiful expression of human life and longing." It is a beauty arising from hardship, from truth and authenticity, and from hope.[11]

Poor Man's Blues, or Psalm 40

Bono once called the psalms a blues. He writes, "Abandonment, displacement, is the stuff of my favourite psalms." The psalms contain anger and frustration. The psalms, at least many of them, were written by an artist with a checkered past. No wonder Bono likens the psalms to the blues.

Bono couldn't pass on recording a psalm, "40," on U2's album *War*. The song he recorded, with its ending refrain, "How long? How long to sing this song?" became a staple for closing their concerts, tens of thousands of fans joining their voices in the plea. Psalm 40 does not contain the exact question, "How long?" (the question occurs throughout the psalms, especially punctuating Psalms 13 and 89), but Psalm 40 was a good choice. This psalm might well be titled "Poor Man's Blues." In this psalm, God hears David's cry in the very first verse. This psalm has David singing of woe and destruction, his feet stuck in the miry clay. It also has David singing a new song, a song of praise when he realizes his deliverance by the merciful hands of God. "*I am poor and needy,*" David cries out at the end. "But," he adds, "the Lord takes thought for me."

David serves as a good foil for the blues singers in many ways. He too had his challenges when it came to women. He too killed a man. In fact, unlike Son House's murder in self-defense, David's was in cold blood. David knew what it was like to be on the run. He confronted forces and evils beyond his control. Though king, he spent much of his life a pawn. He never worked a cotton field, but he spent many hours in the menial labor of shepherding. He wept over graves. And David wrote his own version of Son House's "Death Letter Blues." He was a man of sorrow. Some of David's psalms, such as Psalm 32, are introduced as a "maskil." The exact meaning stumps Hebrew scholars, who conjecture that it's a musical or liturgical term. Perhaps, it's the closest word David could find to express the blues. In the maskils, David and other psalmists give expression to their sorrows. Without that expression, their sorrow would have consumed them from within.

If David knew the cathartic power unleashed through the musical expression of sorrow, he also knew the power of confession. Psalm 51 records the ugliness of sin in an unprecedented depth, far surpassing Charley Patton's best efforts at confessing in "Elder Greene's Blues." David exhausts the Hebrew language to describe his sin. And he exhausts the vocabulary of forgiveness and cleansing.

Psalm 51 is a curious text to be included in the biblical canon. Its roots lie in the even more curious story recorded in 2 Samuel 12, the train wreck of David's adulterous affair with Bathsheba and the eventual murder of Uriah as part of the cover-up. It's a curious psalm and story to be included because it so openly depicts David, God's vice-regent on earth, breaking nearly all of the Ten Commandments in one swoop. David rivals Elder Greene in the depths to which he sinks. But, as Psalm 51 comes to a close, David finds mercy. "Lord, have mercy," was his simple plea. God heard him.

David's isn't the only poetry that sounds like the blues. J. I. Packer once called Ecclesiastes "the Gospel Bassoon." Packer explains, "My built-in makeup as an antihype, anti-Pollyanna reality man anchors me in Ecclesiastes' corner, where realism is the name of the game." Packer finds in Ecclesiastes "bassoon gravity" versus "trumpet brilliance." He finds the gospel, only it's the gospel an "octave lower" than the triumphant versions so often heard. Packer is in good company. Melville's *Moby Dick* refers to Ecclesiastes as "the fine hammered steel of woe," calling it among the truest of books.

Blues isn't relegated to Old Testament poetry alone. Paul could rival them if he wanted to.[12] Jim McGahey, a New Testament scholar friend of mine, refers to Paul's riff on the human condition in Romans 7 as the "Wretched Man Blues." Paul, like David, had a checkered past. He was even complicit in murder. Paul too knew of confession, repentance, forgiveness, and redemption, and he often spoke of the hope of heaven. Yet Paul also knew the depths of sin, the depths to which it takes a person, and the struggle in which it entangles us all. From David to Paul, from Son House to Charley Patton, some of the best verse has been written by those who could sing the wretched man blues, those who know what it is to be a man of sorrows. These artists can't blame Adam for all of the sins and sorrows that meet them at seemingly every turn, and neither can we. He might have started it, but we've heaped our fair share of sins on top of Adam's, and we've harvested our fair share of sorrows because of our own doing. Because of that and not in any way despite of it, we confess. We plead for mercy:

> "Oh, Lord, have mercy if you please . . . give our poor hearts ease."

I've Seen Trouble All My Day

With George Clooney in the lead role and Holly Hunter as an elusive leading lady, the success of the movie should not have come as a surprise. But nobody could have imagined the stunning success of the soundtrack to *O Brother, Where Art Thou?* Selling over five million copies, spinning off two sequel albums and concerts, the soundtrack made a song performed by the movie's Soggy Bottom Boys, "I Am a Man of Constant Sorrow," an instantly recognizable tune. The song has a rich history in bluegrass and country blues, sometimes called hillbilly blues. It was first recorded by Dick Burnett, a blind fiddler from Kentucky. In the 1960s, the song was recorded by Bob Dylan, Peter, Paul and Mary, and (even!) Rod Stewart. But the song reached its full potential with the fictitious movie band, the Soggy Bottom Boys. The song is rather playful, with a catchy bass line. The solo is almost comically broken into by the chorus. But the song's lyrics belie its easygoing sound. The themes pervading the blues, themes explored in this chapter and the previous one, overflow the song. There's rambling and rootlessness, betrayal and loss, abandonment and displacement. And there is impending death. And, at the very end, there is hope: "I'll meet you on God's golden shore."

The song starts in Kentucky, but it reads just like the Delta. When the narrator bemoans, "I've seen trouble all my day," it could have been any of the Delta blues musicians' autobiographies. With no friends and no lovers, even the train, the symbol of redemption and freedom, looks to be a problem. "Perhaps," he muses, "I'll die upon this train." This is utter hopelessness—unless for that one last promise that remains, the hope of God's golden shores. So it is with many a psalm. David finds himself chased, abandoned. He even argues with God. But a note of hope resounds throughout. That promised one, the seed, "restores the broken melody of praise." David was not the seed. But then again, neither was David truly *the* man of sorrows. It wasn't blind Dick Burnett. It wasn't Son House. And it wasn't Charley Patton. Perhaps the most surprising plot twist of all time is that the seed who would be the deliverer of a people of sorrows is also the one who himself would bear sorrow, deep and crushing sorrow. The profound truth of David's psalms lies precisely in this fact: *the* Seed who delivers and *the* Man of Sorrows are indeed one and the same. And it is through him that men, and women, of sorrows have hope. It is to him that they ultimately sing their sorrow song. It is to him that they plead for mercy.

How long? How long will we have to continue to sing this sorrow song? The answer is uncertain. But the promise that the song will eventually be heard is certain.

Cotton field, Holly Ridge, Mississippi, site of Charley Patton's grave.

4

Woman of Sorrows

Naomi's Blues

I went away full, but the Lord has brought me
back empty.

Naomi, Ruth 1:21 NRSV

I'm Ma Rainey #2
Mother of Beale Street.
I'm 78 years old.
Ain't never had enough of nothing
and it's too damn late now.
Lillie Mae Glover
Sept. 9, 1906—March 27, 1985

Lillie Mae Glover's tombstone
Elmwood Cemetery,
Memphis, Tennessee

Music fans flock to Memphis, Tennessee. They've got plenty of reasons, starting with Graceland. Additionally, there's Sun Records and the Sun Studio, the place where Sam Phillips made musical history with his stable of young, hungry artists like Graceland's occupant Elvis Aaron Presley, and then Johnny Cash, Jerry Lee Lewis, Roy Orbison, and Carl Perkins. As the historical marker out front announces, both blacks and whites recorded there. Accordingly, Sun's cadre of black musicians includes Rufus Thomas, Howlin' Wolf, B. B. King, and Ike Turner. Turner's "Rocket 88," a song about a car, gets credited as the first rock 'n' roll song. In 1987, as a tribute to the building's legacy, U2 recorded four songs for *Rattle & Hum* with the legendary B. B. King sitting in. Even Senator Trent Lott cut a record at Sun with his college (Ole Miss) quartet—something I learned in a quite unexpected encounter with the senator as he was coming out of the B. B. King Blues Club on Beale Street and we had a moment for conversation. And there's Beale Street. In its past, this was the main street of blues music. In the present, it has everything from Delta blues to Elvis impersonators covering Neil Diamond. There's the Gibson guitar factory, and the Smithsonian-run Rock 'n' Soul Museum. Visitors to the former Lorraine Motel, now the National Civil Rights Museum, will hear the recording of Mahalia Jackson singing Thomas A. Dorsey's "Precious Lord" at King's funeral. As you listen, you realize the profound role music played in the civil rights movement. A few blocks away you can visit Stax studio. "(Sittin' on) The Dock of the Bay" was recorded here—thousands of miles from the California shores the song dreamily evokes. You can also attend services at Full Gospel Church, where you'll not only hear the reverend Al Green sing but, if you have some time, hear him preach. There's plenty to see in this mecca of American country, blues, soul, and rock 'n' roll. But one of the best places to go in Memphis is Elmwood Cemetery.

There stands the statue of Wade H. Bolton, one of the city's richest men in the nineteenth century. He was shot in a duel in 1869. His will left generous sums of money for his former slaves. His executors were ordered to pay out those sums in Confederate money. Even death could not curtail his cruelty. His monument has a life-sized statue standing tall and proud.

Over on the south side there's a rather different tribute. A block of granite, rough-hewn for the most part, bears the title "Slave Monument." The inscription runs:

> Monument to the Slaves, Final resting place of more than three hundred enslaved Africans buried between 1825 and 1865, For a life of toil and bondage, Only as a nameless grave, Awaited thousands of slaves through the South.

Next to the inscription there's an etched figure of a slave kneeling, chained hands clasped in prayer as the face looks longingly to heaven. Beneath the etching appear the lyrics from an old spiritual entitled, "O Freedom":

> And before I be a slave
> I'll be buried in my grave
> And go home to my Lord and be free.

Not too far from the cemetery's front entrance stands the gravestone of Lillie Mae Glover, known as "Ma Rainey #2." The original Gertrude "Ma" Rainey gets credited as the Mother of the Blues, recording over one hundred songs. Lillie Mae Glover didn't record that many songs, certainly not anywhere near the number of her predecessor. The few she did record sold well, providing opportunities for her to tour the Delta and even make it to points north. She humorously recalled appearances in some far-flung northern towns that had never been visited by blacks before. She liked to say the locals thought they were "bears without tails." Though she lived to see the blues revival in the 1960s, "Ma Rainey #2" got overlooked. Her gravestone says it all: "Ain't never had enough of nothing and it's too damn late now."

Walking through Elmwood Cemetery leaves the impression that the blues, this music that rose out of the Delta and came to Memphis in the early decades of the twentieth century before moving on to St. Louis and Chicago and around the world, is the result of tremendous pressure, the exertion of outside forces upon an object over time, resulting in something that is solid and true. The Slave Monument, Lillie Mae Glover's tombstone, even the stately magnolia trees lining the winding drives through the cemetery like so many sentinels attest to this diamond-like quality of the blues. This music emanates from an oppressed, marginalized people who turned to song to voice their sorrow in the hopes of experiencing freedom.

The original song of the oppressed and of society's marginalized predates the Delta blues, extending all the way back to the narratives of the sacred page. Adam and Eve sang the song of the exile as outcasts from Eden. What response did Eve have when the news of Abel's slaying reached her? Joseph too sang the song of the oppressed from a pit and from a jail, as did the children of Israel in Egypt at a time when Joseph was forgotten. The Egyptians "ruthlessly made the people of Israel work as slaves . . . they made their lives bitter." Did the children of Israel turn bricks without straw into a song lyric? Did they pass the day by groaning field hollers? Even once Israel made its way out of Egypt and into the Promised Land, the song of the oppressed reverberated throughout its history, finding poignant expression in the story of a widow, the story of two widows actually, in the book of Ruth. This sorrow song likely found expression in countless widows and orphans. There were many Ruths, many widows and foreigners, in the biblical world. But this is the story that became part of the biblical canon.

"Naomi's Blues"

Typically, the character Ruth gets all the attention by readers of the story, not entirely surprising since the book is named for her. Next in line of getting attention comes Boaz, the symbol of strength and compassion, the alpha male with a sensitive side. And don't forget the baby, Obed. He's the father of Jesse, the father of David, the father of—skipping a bit—Joseph, Mary's betrothed. But the main character in the book is the one who

"Naomi's Blues"

I had nothin',
I had nothin' at all,
So I went to the
    mountain.
I had nothin',
I had nothin' at all,
So I went to the
    mountain,
and death was all I
    found.

I lost, everything,
    everything.
I lost it all.

I said I'm done now,
I said I'm done.
Gonna make my way
    back down.
I said I'm done now,
I said I'm done.
I have nothin' to offer,
Go and leave me all
    alone.

I lost everything,
    everything.
I lost it all.

She kissed me, she kissed
    me,
Wouldn't let go.

"I'll go with you," she
    said,
"I'll go with you," she
    said,
'Just take me off this
    mountain
"When you go."

I lost everything,
    everything.
I lost it all.

There's hope comin' for
    me,
There's hope comin'
    round the bend.
I went away full, I'm
    comin' back empty,
That's what I said.
I went away full, I'm
    comin' back empty,
But there's a child been
    born to my bed.

I lost everything,
    everything.
I lost it all.
But a child's been born
    to my bed.

SJN

89

tends to get overlooked. André LaCocque refers to her as the "central character" to whom the narrative "incessantly relate[s]." She is the story's other widow, the mother-in-law, Naomi. Naomi doesn't merely serve the narrative to set the stage for Ruth. Naomi *is* the story. The Hebrew word for *widow* literally means "unable to speak." Given their low social ranking in the ancient world, widows were without a voice—except in the case of Naomi. She found her voice in this story.[1]

Naomi's sorrow song begins with a double note of distress: it was the time of Judges—not Israel's most stellar moment—and there was a famine in the land (1:1). These clues signal the reader not only that we are in the minor key but also that things are about to get worse. Out of desperation, Naomi and her husband and sons left Bethlehem for Moab. Over ten years, two marriages, and three deaths later, she returned with her daughter-in-law, who was clinging to her like a burr to a dress. When Naomi returned she met up with her old friends. These women of Bethlehem function like the chorus in a Greek play, moving the narrative along. They show up here and they'll show up again at the end. They asked, "Is this Naomi?" Naomi rebuked them: No longer call me Naomi, which means pleasant, but call me Mara, meaning bitter. Then she peeled off a blues lyric:

I went away full, and I came back empty.

The fuller version of the actual text, compared to my pared down version, reads, "and the Lord has brought me back empty" (Ruth 1:21). There may not be a more honest statement of the human condition. Naomi was devoid not only of possessions, but also of relationships. Even though she had Ruth, she felt the pangs of loneliness. Dietrich Bonhoeffer once said, "A great loneliness has descended upon our age." As part of life under the curse, we're all empty, we're all under this dark cloud of loneliness. Despite our "connected" age of technology, perhaps we are at this time in history more disconnected, more lonely than ever before. In our age of abundance and plenty, we are, with equal irony, more empty than ever before. We're just good at camouflaging or anesthetizing ourselves to our emptiness and loneliness. It takes a widow, one who has had everything stripped away, to tell the truth. A blues pianist from Florida, Ida Goodson, offers, "I don't know, it's just something about it—a woman can always sing the blues better than a man can."[2]

It's worth lingering a bit over Naomi's statement, uncomfortable as that may be. She reminds us of something that we have lost in our age. That thing we have lost is to reflexively think of ourselves as empty, as under the curse. What Naomi said of herself is precisely what happened at Eden, what happened to Adam and Eve, and what is true of all of Adam and Eve's sons and daughters. In the garden, Adam and Eve were full. Now they are empty. So is Naomi. So are we. This declaration of emptiness made by Naomi should be said by all of us.

I Just Can't Keep from Crying

So many blues men and women knew this emptiness all too well. Being black in the South in the pre–civil rights era tended to qualify one as oppressed or marginalized. In "Moanin' Blues," Lightnin' Hopkins can't wait to "cross over that Mason-Dixon Line," even at the cost of "leavin' that good girl behind." Allan Dwight Callahan, in *The Talking Book: African Americans and the Bible,* argues quite persuasively that the themes of exile and exodus ricochet throughout the richly textured culture of African Americans—their stories, their rituals, their music—precisely because their own experiences mirrored the experiences in the sacred book. "African Americans are the children of slavery in America," Callahan begins, adding, "And the Bible, as no other book, is the book of slavery's children." The Bible talked to them, a trope that appears throughout African American lore. The trope partly arises from the widespread illiteracy among slaves—but only partly. The Bible talked to them because in its pages they heard their own story; the Bible gave voice both to their nightmares, the bitter song of slavery, and to their dreams, the hopeful note of redemption, of exodus. The Bible tells the story of an oppressed people, heard loudly and clearly by an oppressed people. Wilma Anne Bailey makes the connection clear: "The Ancient Israelites and the enslaved Africans in the United States, two communities of disparate time and place, found a connection in a common experience of slavery, loss of a homeland, exile, and assaults on their sense of identity and dignity." Bailey adds, "And they adopted the same methods of expressing their grief, laments set to music."[3]

But even among this oppressed group of Southern African Americans there were some even more disadvantaged. This dynamic was also tragically at work in the biblical narrative of Ruth. In times of famine everyone suffers, but then there are the widows and orphans, who suffer more deeply still. Unlike Lightnin' Hopkins's narrator in "Moanin' Blues," who was able to leave, not everyone can just walk away from a situation. Since few opportunities other than physical labor awaited most blacks in this time and place, those unfit for it were driven to the margins of the already marginalized. Among them were the blind. Paul Oliver makes the case that there's such a roster of blind blues artists because they had no other means of survival. While not well suited for physical labor, they could strum a guitar as others worked. They could stand on a street corner or perch on a crate in front of a store and play for change. And many of them excelled. The long list of blind blues legends includes Blind Blake, Blind Lemon Jefferson, Blind Willie McTell, Blind Joe Taggart, and the Five Blind Boys of Alabama, just to name a few. More recently one thinks of Ray Charles. These artists gave voice to sorrow, perhaps of such depths that even the best of other blues musicians could not. Take this lyric from William "Blind Willie" McTell:

Ever since my mother died and left me all alone,
Ever since my mother died and left me all alone,
All my friends have forsaken me, people I haven't
even got no home.

McTell puts the matter succinctly, "My life has been a dog-gone curse."[4]

To this list of artists, I would add Blind Willie Johnson. While revered as a musician, there are likely not many who would label Blind Willie Johnson a theologian. But I certainly would. Willie Johnson was born with sight in Marlin, Texas, in 1902. While he was still quite young, his mother died and his father remarried. When Willie Johnson was seven, his stepmother, seeking revenge after a fight with his father, threw lye into his face, blinding him. Unable to work the fields, Blind Willie Johnson took up a guitar, playing for the rows of share-croppers picking their way through the cotton fields. He recorded only gospel, but in a style that was all blues. He made his first recordings at age twenty-five, "Mother's Children Have a Hard Time," among them. One of his most famous recordings, "Lord, I Just Can't Keep from Cryin' Sometimes," was cut in a hotel in Texas. In his inimitable raspy voice he sang:

When my heart is full of sorrow
When my eyes are filled with tears
Lord, I just can't keep from cryin' sometimes.

There is a raw authenticity here that isn't always found in a world that prefers happy endings. Blind Willie Johnson, the other blind artists, and even Naomi just couldn't keep from crying sometimes.[5]

Blind Willie Johnson's music embodies the convergence of the spirituals and the blues. As mentioned in chapter 1, the symbiosis between these two genres often is overlooked by those who dichotomize them as church music versus the devil's music. Most blues singers, even those bent on being the devil's handmaid, still have the spirituals in them. They can't escape from the clutches of the church. In the case of Blind Willie Johnson, who vowed to record only spirituals, the reverse is true. Try as he might, he couldn't shake the blues. It's a good thing he didn't, for the blues made him a better theologian, especially a better theologian of the minor key. The blues permeates Johnson's music, and not just in terms of musical style. His slide-guitar sound, the twelve-bar rhythms betray his seclusion in the church, revealing the extent of his influences. Though he recorded spirituals, he likely sang many a blues song. Even in his recordings he could not suppress the blues. There is no sentimentality in Blind Willie Johnson. He could, with a note of triumph, declare himself to be "a child of God," who is "going to see the king." He could also, with a note of clear-eyed realism, declare that mother's children, who also happen to be God's children, have a hard time. The song alluded to here is titled "Mother's Children Have a Hard Time," but the lyric runs "motherless children have a hard time." The song is an anthem for the orphan. It's also a bit of memoir for Johnson. Though he had a stepmother, Johnson considered himself much like an orphan, and rightly so given what happened to him. He filled his songs with longing anticipation of reuniting with his mother in the world to come.

Blind Lemon Jefferson added more depth to this sense of abandonment when he cried out, "I am motherless, fatherless, sister and brotherless too" in "Broke and Hungry." Blind Lemon Jefferson was born in Couchman, Texas, in 1897 (some accounts say1887). The flat terrain stretches for miles, but, being born blind, Lemon Jefferson couldn't see any of it. By his adolescence he sang and played guitar. By 1926 he had earned enough of a reputation to score a recording session with Paramount. Jefferson, too, felt the pinch of the blues versus the spirituals. He recorded blues under his name, while he recorded spirituals under the moniker Deacon L. J. Bates. The L, J, and B are a clever but obvious rearrangement of the initials of his blues name. Both his spirituals and his blues were distributed widely, but it's his blues recordings of typical themes that have become well-regarded and reissued classics. His recording of the blues standard "Match Box Blues" is the most anthologized, along with "Black Snake Moan." An obvious double entendre, this title was recently borrowed to title a movie. His recordings tell the expected blues tales of love lost and loneliness. "Broke and Hungry," "Rambler Blues," and "Lemon's Worried Blues" all lament his misfortunes. "Lord, I'm worried here, worried everywhere I go," he cries.

Blind Lemon Jefferson also sang songs of what amounts to social protest. His "Rising High Water Blues" chronicles the impact of the 1927 Mississippi River flood, and his "Boll Weevil Blues" relates the devastation of the destructive insect. But his songs of social protest mostly deal with the injustices of the prison system and the toll excessive punishment took. Songs like "Blind Lemon's Penitentiary Blues," "'Lectric Chair Blues," and "Hangman's Blues" resonate with helplessness, and not just for the ones in prison. At the end of "'Lectric Chair Blues," the loved one left behind moans, "I feel like jumping in the ocean, I feel like jumping in the sea/There wasn't no blood in my heart, and they brought my electrocuted daddy to me." Yet Blind Lemon Jefferson never fully lost his hope. In "See That My Grave Is Kept Clean," he declares directly, "I believe what the Bible told." Blind Lemon Jefferson made his last recordings in 1929, and as with other blues musicians, mystery surrounds his death with many conflicting reports. The most likely seems to be that he suffered a heart attack while caught outside and alone in the middle of the night during a bitter Chicago storm. He was in Chicago to record and was likely on his way to or from playing for a party. Jefferson was far from the fields of west Texas when he froze to death in the streets of Chicago. Ironically, his death recalled what he sang in "See That My Grave Is Kept Clean":

> Well, my heart stopped beating and my hands turned
>   cold,
> My heart stopped beating and my hands turned cold,
> Now I believe what the Bible told.[6]

Blind Willie Johnson and Blind Lemon Jefferson could voice their complaint, clothed in honesty and humility, to God, as did the psalmist, as did Naomi. These complaints arise from the misfortunes of life that each of these "musicians" experienced. Some misfortunes came from the hands of malicious people, some from the new "normal" that governs a fallen world. Samuel Charters and Paul Oliver, in their respective studies, have called the blues a complaint. Angela Y. Davis thinks that isn't strong enough. She prefers to see the blues, especially those blues sung by the great blues women or the songs mentioned above recorded by Blind Lemon Jefferson, as protest, as the "impassioned denunciation of injustice." She might be right. They experienced something, or many things as the case may be, and they wanted to do something about it. Or, better, they wanted someone to do something about it. As we saw in an earlier chapter, the interpolation "Oh, Lord" isn't just filler in the blues. Hermann Gunkel's study of the Psalms reveals that the lament, the biblical "blues," was not uttered in hopeless situations. The psalmist lamented precisely at those times when the Lord's intervention could make a difference. Naomi's complaint (protest?) in chapter 1 doesn't end the story. We the readers of the story are left at the end of chapter 1 waiting with Naomi for some intervention.[7]

The Time of the Barley Harvest

Though Naomi was blue, she was resourceful. The text of Ruth tells us that it was the time of the barley harvest (1:22), and that Naomi had a relative (2:1). Naomi's blues song sounds a note of hope. Kirsten Nielsen observes that chapter 1 of Ruth ends with a "stage direction aimed at both Naomi and Ruth," a stage direction that points to potential and promise. We all know how the story unfolds. Girl meets boy, they fall in love, and boy goes down to the town gate, and someone takes his sandal off, and then there's a wedding. Some of the details may be a bit unique, but otherwise it's a classic love story. All of this is incidental to what the narrator of the story wants to tell us in chapter 4, as the focus shifts off of Boaz and Ruth, the characters in the classic love story, and back on the widow. "A son has been born to Naomi," sings the chorus of the neighborhood women as they return to the stage (4:17 NRSV). The son was her redeemer, her restorer. Naomi was empty, and she was made full. These were good times, but they didn't come cheaply.[8]

Here we may linger a bit, too. Naomi reminds us not only to embrace the curse, but also to embrace the cross. As the chorus of women sang to Naomi of the son, so the angels would say to the shepherds, "For unto you is born this day in the City of David a savior, which is Christ the Lord" (Luke 2:10–11 KJV). Here is the seed, the son, the redeemer, who makes those who are empty full, and makes those who are bitter pleasant. This son, the text outlines, will be to Naomi a redeemer (4:14), a restorer of life (4:15), and a nourisher for her old age (4:15). Of the middle term, "restorer," Katherine Doob Sakenfield notes, "The verb here translated 'to restore' means more literally to 'bring back.' It is exactly the verb that Naomi used in her words to the women in 1:21, expressing her despairing perception that the Lord had brought her back empty." Sakenfield also points to the ironic twist of the use of this same word in 4:15: "Now the Lord is blessed for the reversal of Naomi's situation. Emptiness has become fullness."[9]

There are a number of ironic twists in this book of Ruth, not the least of which concerns the role of women. In Old Testament Hebrew culture the father names the child. In this case the women of Bethlehem name him (4:17). In Old Testament Hebrew culture widows carried little social clout. In this case Naomi dominates the story. Any number of commentators and Old Testament scholars use this subversive story for all sorts of agendas. Let me add yet another. This story focuses on these women because of Ida Goodson's observation that "a woman can always sing the blues better than a man can."

This book is Naomi's blues. She, and the women's chorus, should have the stage.

"Tain't Nobody's Bizness If I Do"

Ida Goodson's observation may ring true on a number of levels. The highest-paid black entertainer in America during the 1920s was blues woman Bessie Smith. In 1902, a year before W. C. Handy "discovered" the blues on a railroad platform in Tutwiler, Mississippi, Gertrude "Ma" Rainey took the stage performing the blues before audiences. Smith and Rainey made no fewer than 252 recordings between them. Add Billie Holiday and many others, and the predominance of women blues singers becomes quite clear. Not only *can* these women sing the blues better than men, in many respects they did.

Gertrude Pridgett, born in 1886 in Georgia, became "Ma Rainey" when she married William "Pa" Rainey in 1904. She had already been performing in early vaudeville acts and minstrel shows on her own. She and her husband were known as the "Assassinators of the Blues." By the 1910s she was touring throughout the South with the popular act Rabbit Foot Minstrels. She finally had her first studio session in 1923. Rainey made up for lost time, racking up over a hundred recordings in just a brief six-year stretch. She continued touring until 1933, and in 1939 she died of a heart attack in her Georgia home. Like all blues singers, she sang of love lost and of cruel lovers—it's just that in her case, the mistreaters were the men. Most of Ma Rainey's songs have her getting the blues at night because her man has left her and gone after another woman, as in the case of "These All Night Long Blues." In one song she strategizes, "Going to buy me a bulldog to watch me while I sleep/To keep my man from making his midnight creep." These love songs constitute, according to Sandra Lieb, but one of three categories of songs by Ma Rainey. The other two categories include lighthearted songs, like "Barrel House Blues," and songs of a much more cynical nature. Lieb describes this latter group as songs that "display what we would now call an absurdist sense of frustration at trying to decipher an increasingly baffling world." These would be songs of complaint, verging on protest.[10]

Ma Rainey's protest songs concerned the cruelties experienced in sharecropper life. She too recorded a song about the boll weevil. And her protest songs dealt with jail, the old themes of crime and punishment. In "Cell Bound Blues," the song's narrator finds herself bound for a prison cell because she killed her man in a fight. We come to find out in the course of the song, however, that she killed him in self-defense:

> My man walked in and begin to fight
> I took my gun in my right hand, said,
> "Hold him, folks, I don't wanta kill my man."
> When I did that, he hit me 'cross my head
> First shot I fired, my man fell dead.

In her case, a woman's case, pleading self-defense won't work, so the song's narrator is off to jail. In "Chain Gang Blues," a song that was cowritten with Thomas A. Dorsey before he turned to writing spirituals, a "poor gal" is "in trouble." We need to remember the world in which she was performing these songs. Women had just won the right to vote in the 1920s. Instead of finding clemency, this "poor gal" faces:

> Many days of sorrow, many nights of woe
> Many days of sorrow, many nights of woe
> And a ball and chain, everywhere I go.

These jail songs of hers were not autobiographical. Unlike Son House, or even a later Johnny Cash, Ma Rainey never spent even one night in a prison cell. She was simply singing for those who did. She was especially singing for Southern black women, who had little if any social standing. The final song of hers that we will consider here, though, is autobiographical. In "Countin' the Blues," she recalls the places she sang in, like Memphis's Beale Street. She remembers "sittin' on the Southern," the train that she would "ride all night long" as she toured all through the South. She also brings to mind certain songs such as her very first recording, "Bad Luck Blues." These were all "good songs," she fondly remembers. But while those were good songs, good memories, she ends the song on a downbeat:

> Lord, going to sleep, boys, mama's just now got bad
> news
> Lord, going to sleep now, just now I got bad news
> Try to dream away my troubles, countin' these blues.

Most likely she's referring to the news she just received of her weak heart, a weak heart that would cause her to stop singing and eventually would give out. What is most telling in this song, however, is the beginning. Once the instruments start up, but before she starts singing, Ma Rainey solemnly speaks these lines: "Lord, I got the blues this mornin'/I want everybody to go down in prayer, Lord, Lord." She not only offers a prayer, but, as Angela Davis insightfully puts it, "Rainey consciously refigures the blues as prayer." Faced with a desperate situation, she turned to lament, to the blues. Following the lead of Gunkel, she did not turn to lament because she was hopeless, but because she counted on divine intervention.[11]

Sterling Brown memorialized what Ma Rainey and her music meant to the South in his 1932 poem "Ma Rainey." In the first two stanzas, Brown tells how the poor folks come from all around to hear Ma Rainey. They come from the little river settlements, from corn rows, and from lumber camps. They come with their "aches an' miseries." By the third stanza of the poem, Ma Rainey takes the stage:

> O Ma Rainey,
> Sing yo' song;

Now you's back,
Whah you belong,
Git way inside us,
Keep us strong . . .
O Ma Rainey,
Li'l an' low;
Sing us 'bout de hard luck
Roun' our do';
Sing us 'bout de lonesome road
We mus' go . . .

In the last stanza, Brown has Ma Rainey singing "Backwater Blues," another song recalling the 1927 Mississippi River flood. When the audience, those poor folks who came from the little towns, heard it, "dey natchally bowed dey heads an' cried." "I want everyone to go down in prayer, Lord, Lord," Ma Rainey sang in "Countin' the Blues." As Sterling Brown has it, when she gave her blues concerts in the juke joints and in the barrel houses, they did go down in prayer, bowing their heads and crying from the depths of their souls.[12]

Ma Rainey is called the Mother of the Blues not only because she was the first to sing them. She also earned that rank because she influenced that entire first generation of female blues singers. Not the least among that generation stands Bessie Smith. She's been called "The Empress of the Blues." Born in Chattanooga, Tennessee, on April 15, 1894, Bessie Smith would soon be an orphan. Her father, an itinerant Baptist minister, died just after she was born, and her mother passed away a few years later. Little else is known of her before she turned eighteen. In that year, the Moses Stokes Troupe passed through town. Anxious to get out and move on, Bessie auditioned, landing a role as a dancer. At the time, the lead singer of the troupe was Ma Rainey. It was Rainey who would mentor Smith and bring her to the microphone. Bessie Smith would soon surpass her mentor. While Ma Rainey had dominated the South, Bessie Smith dominated both the North and the South. Like Rainey, Smith took many opportunities to sing on behalf of those who had no voice; as Christopher John Farley captures it, "She raised the spirits of the downtrodden simply by lifting her voice." And what a voice she had to lift! Farley describes her voice first as a boxer, but then corrects himself, as "perhaps boxing is too inelegant a term for the melodious precision with which she spun out her songs."[13]

Boxing, however, may still be a good way to describe her singing. Early attempts at recording were not met with success. Thomas Edison himself reviewed one of her attempts, rating it "NG" for no good, and she was repeatedly told her voice was "too rough." Eventually, though, the executives at Columbia took a different stance. She cut the first of what would be about 160 recordings with Columbia in 1923, the same year as Ma Rainey. The boxing allusion works well on a much deeper level, however. Sidney Bechet said of Bessie Smith that "the trouble was inside her and she wouldn't let it rest." A young Mahalia Jackson heard that trouble. "When I was a little girl," the future queen of gospel recalled, "I felt she was having troubles like me. That's why it was such a comfort for the people of the South to hear her. She expressed something they couldn't put into words."[14]

Bessie Smith sang often of love, but she also sang her share of social protest. She too sang of the ravages of the 1927 Mississippi River flood in "Back Water Blues" and of the injustices of the penal system in songs like "Jail House Blues." She could also sing of the plight of the orphan:

> No father to guide me, no mother to care
> Must bear my troubles all alone
> Not even a brother to help me share
> This burden I must bear alone.

But the issue that most often caused her to step into the ring was poverty and the challenges faced by the poor. In "Washwoman's Blues," she put the drudgery of the work to song:

> Me and my ole washboard sho' do have some cares
> and woes
> Me and my ole washboard sho' do have some cares
> and woes
> In the muddy water, wringin' out these dirty clothes.

"All day long I'm slavin', " she adds.

She offered what might amount to an anthem for the poor in "Poor Man's Blues." "Mr. rich man rich man," she thunders, "open your heart and mind/Give a poor man a chance, help stop these hard times." The song ends with these troubling lines:

> Poor man fought all the battles, poor man would
> fight again today
> He would do anything you ask him, in the name of
> the USA
> Now the war is over, poor man must live same as you
> If it wasn't for the poor man, mister rich man what
> would you do?

Though explicitly addressing the issue of poverty, Smith was also decrying racism. In fact, Angela Davis's intensive study of her music concludes that her songs "articulate a consciousness that takes into account social conditions of class exploitation, racism, and male dominance." Davis further contends that this consciousness, nursed by these songs, would eventually turn into activism, the activism of the civil rights movement. In *A Bad Woman Feeling Good: Blues and the Women Who Sing Them*, Buzzy Jackson observes, "Smith's songs were important early sounds in the twentieth century struggle for black civil rights." Not surprisingly, then, writer Ralph Ellison prefers to call Bessie Smith, not the "Empress of the Blues," but "Priestess of the Blues." Bessie Smith died in 1937 in a car accident just outside Clarksdale, Mississippi. She was taken to the colored hospital, where she was pronounced dead. She was buried in Philadelphia, in the North.[15]

One other familiar voice among these early blues women belonged to Billie Holiday. Though she might be better classified as a jazz musician, "Lady Day" or just "Lady," as she was called, both lived and sang the blues. Hilton Als exclaims, "She couldn't help seeing what was wrong and saying something about it." One of the most controversial things she talked about was lynching, in the song *Time* magazine declared the best song of the century, "Strange Fruit." *Time* was doing some penance. Back in 1939, when the song first came out, the magazine dismissed it as mere propaganda for the NAACP. The strange fruit hanging from southern trees that the song hauntingly speaks of is a "Black body swinging in the southern breeze."[16]

The song was first a poem written by Abel Meeropol. He gave it to Billie Holiday after he heard her sing in a club in Harlem. She first performed it as a song in 1938, before recording it in 1939. Meeropol wrote the poem after he saw a photograph of a lynching in 1930. Another lynching, that of Rubin Stacey in Fort Lauderdale, Florida, in 1935, captured national attention. That year the Costigan-Wagner bill was introduced to the U.S. Congress; it would have made lynching illegal and would have punished sheriffs and judges who allowed mobs to carry out lynching. It was defeated. Estimates vary, but somewhere around 3,000 Southern blacks were lynched from the years immediately after the Civil War until the 1930s. While some of these may have been for capital offenses, more often than not the offenses were minor or, worse yet, imaginary. Regardless of the offense, all of these cases were mob violence and utter travesties of justice.[17]

When Billie Holiday sang "Strange Fruit," it was often met with eerie responses by the audience. It's a song that leaves one wanting to sigh or repent, not to clap. David Margolick recalls the performance of the song at the Apollo Theater in Harlem, retelling the story by Jack Schiffman, whose family ran the Apollo. When you heard the song before, Schiffman wrote in his memoirs, "you might have been touched and nothing more. . . . But at the Apollo, the song took on profound intimations." Schiffman continues, "You saw in Billie Holiday the wife or sister or mother of one of the victims beneath the tree, almost prostrate with sorrow and fury." But then Schiffman reveals that the audience saw something far more, "You even saw and felt the agony of another lynching victim, this one suspended from a wooden cross at Calvary."[18] These sorrow songs, songs of complaint and protest, longed for divine intervention. And those who sang them, as well as those who listened to them, knew that there was One who could hear their song, because he too once sang it.

Etta James, of the second generation of blues women, entitled her autobiography *Rage to Survive*. Having met with some success, she no longer needs to rage to survive, but she still feels the need to rage: "I'm using my power to turn my passion and pain into song; I wanna go back to the studio and rage a little more." And with that rage she declares, "I still got a lot more songs to sing." These women—Ma Rainey, Bessie Smith, Billie Holiday, Etta James, and many others—sang for the women, and for the men, who couldn't. They expressed their sorrow, and in their shared experience they found a measure of relief. But it would take more than a song to bring them the true freedom they desired. It would take a singer, *the Singer*, who could sing the song of redemption to set the captive free.[19]

How the Blues Saved My Soul

This longing for freedom, for deliverance, has echoed through the sorrow songs down the millennia. Returning to the story of Naomi, at the end of chapter 1 and the beginning of chapter 2, the narrative moves from desperation and towards hope. The two signals were the barley harvest (1:22) and the relative that Naomi had. Naomi knew the barley harvest to be but a short-term fix, which is why the words, "now Naomi had a relative" (2:1 NIV) become the point on which the whole narrative turns. This little phrase holds the long-term answer to Naomi's dilemma. The relative she thought she was talking about was Boaz, and then eventually, after that sandal thing, Obed. The redemption, restoration, and nourishment that the chorus of women sang of in chapter 4, however, far transcends anything Obed could bring to the life of this formerly empty widow. The narrative points us beyond Obed, even beyond David. The narrative points us to the One hanging from a cross on Calvary.

Naomi's blues lyric in chapter 1 (1:21) is best understood Adamically. In other words, in order for the fullest meaning of "I went away full, and I came back empty" to be heard and understood, one must hear in it the plight of Adam and all his posterity along with him. This is the song of emptiness that we in our collective humanity sing, or at least the song we should be singing.

The lyric sung by the chorus of women in chapter 4 (4:14–15), triumphantly declares Naomi's redemption may be heard in its fullest sense only when one hears Christ within it. If Naomi's lyric in chapter 1 takes us back to Genesis 3, this lyric of the women in chapter 4 takes us to Luke 2: "For unto you is born this day in the city of David a Savior, which is Christ the Lord." This Christocentric, or better to say Christotelic, reading of Ruth 4 is the only reading that explains why this story, among the countless stories of widows and orphans, makes it into the biblical canon. In fact, this story becomes the story of the biblical canon in miniature. This storyline may be plotted as having everything (creation), losing everything (the fall and the curse), and having everything restored (the cross, redemption, and recreation). This is the story that stretches from the first human being, Adam, until the final human being, the God-Man, Christ (1 Cor. 15). It is Christ who redeems, restores, and nourishes. It is Christ who brings fullness to Adam's emptiness. He sings for the captive. He is the one who ultimately restores widows and orphans and those weeping in the shadows of southern trees.

As the Book of Ruth comes to a close, Naomi's blues come full circle, precisely because of Christ. And, for that matter, so does the repertoire of Blind Willie Johnson, and again precisely because of Christ. Johnson not only recorded "Lord, I Just Can't Keep from Cryin' Sometime," but also recorded song after song testifying to the promise and hope of redemption, never losing his faith. Chief among these is "I Know His Blood Can Make Me Whole." Again, the Seed, the Son, who brings redemption. All it takes is to touch the hem of his garment. Blind Willie Johnson likely recalled that episode from the Gospels many times, the scene where the woman, an outcast, with a dire need and an outstretched hand needed simply to touch the hem of Christ's garment as he passed by. Johnson memorialized this woman in his song:

> I was sick and I couldn't get well,
> I was sick and I couldn't get well.
> I just touched the hem of his garment.

Christ makes the empty full, the sick well, and he causes the blind to see. This is no prosperity gospel. Blind Willie Johnson's life too clearly illustrates that it's not a world of blue skies and happy times. Johnson died in 1947. His house caught fire and, though attempts were made to put it out, burned to the ground. With nowhere to go, Johnson spent the night in the ruins, covered in wet blankets and wet newspapers. Due to the evening's chill, Johnson caught pneumonia and died shortly thereafter. Ironically, Johnson's death reflects his most well-known song, "Dark Was the Night, Cold Was the Ground," a "wordless monody of moans accompanied by a restless, singing slide [guitar]." This song, alongside the music of Bach and Beethoven, was launched into outer space in 1977 on board the spaceship *Voyager*. The song recalls Christ's death and his burial in the tomb. It is a song of Good Friday, a song that cries out for Resurrection Sunday. Other recorded versions of it have words. Blind Willie Johnson, so moved by the event of which he sang, couldn't put words to it. He let the guitar speak as his voice moaned.[20]

The stillness of Good Friday scares us. The immobile Redeemer, pierced and scarred and shut up in death, is too much for us. We prefer "Up from the grave He arose with a mighty triumph o'er his foes," and rightly so. But failing to linger at Good Friday, failing to keep Good Friday as an essential piece of our senses diminishes and distorts the full weight of Christ's work. If we don't linger at Good Friday, we have no hope to offer those who suffer from great floods, or from injustices, or from any of the litany of curses in the fallen world. Without Good Friday there is nothing left to say to those left mourning in the shadow of swaying bodies hanging from trees. And without Good Friday, that dark, cold night, there would be no redemption. Because there *is* Good Friday, there is something to say to those under the curse. Because of Good Friday there is the redemption and the fullness Blind Willie Johnson sang of. It is the redemption and freedom that *the Child* brings to the sons and daughters of Adam.

There are various types of Christ in the Book of Ruth—Boaz as the kinsman-redeemer, and Obed as the seed and the son. But there is another type, the archetype of humanity. In the widow Naomi we see what it means to be human. Her blues song is truly the song of humanity, replete with the rhythms of the curse, but thankfully also the rhythms of the cross. The answer to Naomi's sorrow song came through the unlikely presence of an infant, life in the midst of death, hope in the midst of desperation, fullness in the midst of emptiness. "Today there has been born to you in the city of David," that king whose great-grandmother was the foreigner Ruth, "a deliverer—the Messiah, the Lord" (Luke 2:11, REB). When the shepherds, a marginalized group in that time and place, heard these words, the angels were talking about an infant. This infant became the Man of Sorrows who hears the complaint and protest of both men and women of sorrow. He hears, he intervenes, and he gives them freedom.

Painted advertisement,
Billups Plantation commissary window.

5

Precious Lord

Harmonizing the Curse and the Cross

> I am tired, I am weak, I am worn . . . Precious
> Lord, Take my hand.
>
> Thomas A. Dorsey

> My God, my God, why have you forsaken me?
>
> Matthew 27:46 NRSV

He lived two lives, and for these two lives he had two personas. The one was Barrelhouse Tom or Georgia Tom Dorsey, a bluesman who held sway in the 1920s, playing the piano for Ma Rainey and arranging and writing songs for her and many others. In the same period, this blues pianist teamed up with Tampa Red, on the slide guitar, making for a formidable blues duo. Tampa Red, born Hudson Whittaker in Georgia, was raised in Tampa before he, like Georgia Tom, migrated north to Chicago. Then in 1930, the persona of Barrelhouse Tom/Georgia Tom gave way to the one that would become much more famous, that of Thomas A. Dorsey, composer and writer of gospel, or as most prefer, the "father of gospel." It might be better, however, not to consider the two personas as two distinct and separate lives. Instead, Barrelhouse Tom and Thomas A. Dorsey might best be considered as one, albeit extremely complex, life.[1]

In his study of the development of gospel music, Don Cusic explains Dorsey's success in crystallizing the movement of black gospel by pointing to Dorsey's "subconscious" use of blues. Dorsey, Cusic argues, "used the blues form in his melodies and his decidedly gospel lyrics were aimed at the poor and the outcast." Dorsey knew that the kingdom of God belonged to such as these, the poor and the outcast, because Dorsey was one of them. His blues had taught him as much.[2]

Mary Had a Baby

In his landmark work, *Jesus and the Disinherited*, Howard Thurman isn't long into writing his book when, after observing that there are many interpretations of Jesus, he declares, "But few of these interpretations deal with what the teachings and the life of Jesus have to say to those who stand, at a moment in human history, with their backs against the wall." Thurman revealed in the second sentence what he was up to in his book. Christianity was born, Thurman rolls on, in a cauldron of persecution and suffering. It emerged among the weak and the defenseless. Thurman makes his point by gently reminding his readers that Jesus was born a poor Jew, under Roman occupation. Jesus was socially and politically disinherited. He was born on, and he lived on, the margins.[3]

Before Thurman wrote his book, the old Negro spirituals offered the same argument, not by sophisticated means but, seemingly, by instinct. The communities from which these spirituals arose, the slave quarters, the Reconstruction plantations, lumber camps, levee camps, and even prison work gangs, readily identified with the biblical story of the incarnation. As the elements of the story of Jesus's birth are ticked off, the connection resonates deeper: a frightened young girl, a poor couple, poor shepherds, oppressive kings and rulers, a people in bondage. This poor couple was forced to go to the stables, forced to birth a child among the animals, as there was no room for them in the inn. But lurking in these dark melodies is a note of hope, the promise of freedom. Redemption lies in that manger in the stable. "Go tell it on the mountain," runs the ubiquitous spiritual, "that Jesus Christ is born."

In the incarnation, Christ is Emmanuel, God *with us*. The word *sympathy* literally means "with (*sym*) feeling (*pathos*)." But just on the surface. *Pathos* means far more than mere outward expression of feeling. Sympathy isn't, with apologies to Barry Manilow, simply a matter of my feeling sad when you're feeling sad. To be truly sympathetic is to enter in, to take upon oneself the same, the I merging with You and becoming We. The old spiritual captures this sympathy:

> Sister Mary had-a but one child,
> Born in Bethlehem.
> And a-every time that-a baby cried,
> She'd-a rocked him in a weary land,
> She'd-a rocked him in a weary land.

In the event of his birth, Jesus became truly sympathetic to humanity. And as an infant, he was forced to flee for his safety with his family. As the prophet said, "out of Egypt, have I called my son" (Matt. 2:15 NRSV). His life was beginning to take on more and more the story of Israel, indeed the story of all humanity. While Jesus's family became exiles on the run, fleeing for their lives to Egypt, Rachel was weeping for her children (Matt. 2:18). The communities who sang the spirituals connected with all of these elements of the biblical story of Jesus's birth. These communities felt the sympathy of Jesus, for he had entered fully and wholly into a world of suffering and oppression, a world of limits. And as he walked through the world, he touched those "in a weary land." Even the characters that Jesus encountered in the pages of the Gospels became connections for the singers of the spirituals. The woman taken in adultery, the woman at the well, the lame and the blind, and a thief hanging on a cross all resonated with their experience. Jesus was rejected by the religious establishment, even rejected by the crowds of commoners. He never accumulated wealth, seeming to live on very little. He was arrested and tried in what amounted to a mockery of justice. He died a cruel death upon a cross, the lowest form of punishment. He was abandoned by God. He was with pathos, knowing the human condition.

The Gospels are set against the backdrop of a world inhabited by outcasts. As Obery Hendricks observes, "the New Testament clearly portrays Jesus, his family, and, with few exceptions, everyone he encountered throughout his life as impoverished and oppressed, exploited by the religious establishment, brutalized by their Roman colonizers." The singers of the spirituals recognized their own world in the pages of the Gospels. The songs of Jesus became their song. Allen Dwight Callahan, in his study of African American reading of the Bible—what he terms the reading by "slavery's children"—clusters his findings under four categories: exile, symbolizing oppression and the outsider status; exodus, the preeminent theme of bondage and the hope of redemption; Ethiopia, the center of a biblical "cartography of hope"; and Emmanuel. Regarding the latter, Callahan notes, "More than the Lord and God of slavery's children, Jesus is their peer: he is as they are, for he has suffered as they have suffered." James Cone puts it this way: "According to the spirituals, the meaning of Jesus' birth, life, death, and resurrection is found in his identity with the poor, the blind, and the sick. He has

"Prayin' Blues"

Sometimes I feel like cryin',
feel I lost my way.
Sometimes I got nothin'
left to do but pray.

Look down on me, Jesus,
down from heaven above.
Look down on me, Jesus,
send mercy from above.

They say there's somethin' better
just down the new highway.
I just keep movin' on
nowhere for me to stay.

Look down on me, Jesus,
down from heaven above.
Look down on me, Jesus,
send rest from above.

And when I'm cold, lyin' in the grave,
may it say upon my stone,
"Here he lies, someday to rise,
Lord, have mercy on his soul."

Look down on me, Jesus,
down from heaven above.
Look down on me, Jesus,
send peace from above.

SJN

come to set them free." Mary rocked her baby's cradle in a weary land.[4]

Out of Atlanta

Thomas A. Dorsey inhabited a world immersed in this biblical narrative. His father, educated at Morehouse College, was a Baptist minister. His mother was the church organist. It is also true, however, that Dorsey's world was not entirely like that of blues singers from the Delta. Unlike most of the blues artists, especially those in the Delta, Dorsey knew how to read music. There was a greater sophistication in the Dorsey home than in the white clapboard plantation church where the spirituals were stomped out, a greater sophistication than was found among his Delta blues colleagues. Nevertheless, the underlying rhythm of Dorsey's world was the same as theirs. Dorsey grew up in this church and in this ethos. And when Thomas Dorsey came of age, he left the church. He became the prodigal son, yet another story from the Gospels.

Dorsey got his first taste of life outside of the church selling sodas to audiences in Atlanta's 81 Theatre, where he heard Ma Rainey and Bessie Smith, along with other vaudeville performers and comedy acts. Inspired by what he saw and heard, he turned to performing at small parties, playing the imitated piano runs he picked up at the 81. As a budding musician, he found Atlanta to be wanting, and so set off for the North in 1916. Michael Harris notes the pull on Dorsey coming from the campaign launched by Chicago's black newspaper, the *Chicago Defender*, for the "Great Northern Drive." The paper actively promoted this mass exodus of oppressed blacks from the South to the North from 1915 until 1917. That pull was coupled with another, more existential, one for Dorsey. Harris notes that at this point in Dorsey's life, he "barely eked out a living playing piano through the night." Not seeing much of a future for himself in Atlanta, he first went to Indiana, working in a mill and studying music on the side. Then Dorsey made it to Chicago and settled there in 1918.[5]

In his early days in the city, Dorsey studied at the Chicago College of Composition and Arranging. But his own success as a blues pianist stole him away from his studies. Georgia Tom, as he was called by then, took the clubs by storm and began copyrighting what would be the first of many songs. Just as he was beginning his climb, he suffered a setback. Back in Atlanta his mother boarded a train bound for Chicago to bring her son home. Dorsey had experienced the first of what would be two major nervous breakdowns. He weighed a mere 128 pounds when his mother retrieved him. While convalescing in Atlanta, his mother urged a spiritual cure, admonishing him to return to the church. Dorsey thought his fortunes lay elsewhere, returning to Chicago and the blues scene as soon as he recovered. While his first stint met with only a modicum of success, this second venture to the Windy City would eventually be a triumph.[6]

Despite his running from his mother's urging to return to the church, Dorsey did have a religious epiphany in that same year of 1921. His uncle, no doubt commissioned by his mother, convinced him to attend the National Baptist Convention meeting in Chicago in September. At the convention Dorsey witnessed what amounted to a religious carnival. He even had to pay admission. But at the convention, he also heard W. M. Nix debut his song "I Do, Don't You?" from the new songbook for the National Baptist Convention, *Gospel Pearls*. Biographer Michael Harris explains the effect on Dorsey: "Whatever example, admonition, and even illness had been unable to accomplish in the cause of Dorsey's religious development, the fervency and expressive quality of Nix's singing that Sunday morning did." For the first time Dorsey was hearing gospel music, the genre he himself would come to perfect. Dorsey later recalled the moment: "My inner being was thrilled. My soul was a deluge of divine rapture."

And like most attendees at a revival meeting, Dorsey found himself making a commitment that morning. He would apply his talents to songwriting for the kingdom. There would be no more blues. Georgia Tom would give way to Thomas A. Dorsey. [7]

Dorsey's revival meeting commitment, however, was short-lived. He did write a gospel song, copyrighted on September 11, 1922—a full calendar year later. The song made it into the second edition of *Gospel Pearls*. But he found that the blues came much more easily. Before long, he was back in the clubs of Chicago, and soon his band would be enlisted to tour with Ma Rainey. He was writing songs and arranging music for her, for Bessie Smith, and for a roster of blues singers. His star was rising again. By 1926, however, Dorsey hesitated, feeling the internal pressure to return to making church music. Once again he became Thomas A. Dorsey. Clothed in this persona, however, he met financial difficulty. Then he teamed up with Tampa Red and staggered back to the blues. In 1928, the duo produced "It's Tight Like That," a song of obvious sexual overtones. That one song brought Dorsey more money than he usually saw in a year.

It was also in 1928 that he experienced his second breakdown. Success just might have proven too much, or maybe it was that inner pressure. Regardless, after this recovery, he vowed that he was finished with the blues, no matter how financially beneficial they were to him. Allowing for a minor "relapse" in 1931, during which he recorded some great blues, from 1928 on until his death in 1993, the persona Georgia Tom did indeed give way to that of Thomas A. Dorsey. In 1932 he began his long stint as choir director at Pilgrim Baptist Church in Chicago, established a publishing house for African American gospel sheet music, and formed the National Convention of Gospel Choirs and Choruses. In that same year he wrote what would become his signature song, "Precious Lord, Take My Hand." The song came at a horrendous personal cost for Dorsey. He had just arrived in St. Louis to do a gospel concert, when he read a telegram urging him to come home immediately. His wife, near the end of her first pregnancy, fell extremely ill. By the time he made it home, his wife had died, just after she managed to give birth. His son died two days later. Friends arranged for him to stay in a room with a piano for a time of recovery. After days of seclusion he sat down and wrote:

> Precious Lord, take my hand,
> Lead me on, let me stand,
> I am tired, I am weak, I am worn;
> Through the storm, through the night,
> Lead me on to the light.
> Take my hand, precious Lord,
> Lead me home.

Thomas Dorsey once said that there are "moanin' blues" that are used in the spirituals. Was he thinking of his own music?[8]

Dorsey also said that there are spirituals in the "moanin' blues." Again, his own blues are no exception. There are the songs replete with the double entendres, like "Pig Meat Blues" and the previously mentioned "It's Tight Like That." There are also songs that skip any pretense whatsoever. In "Come on In," Dorsey sounds like a frat boy: "Let's get drunk and have one good time/Take off your shirt, hang it on the chair. . . . I'm drunk and disorderly, I don't care/If you want to, you can pull off your underwear." How ironic that this lyric was written by the same person who wrote "Precious Lord." Famed American historian Martin E. Marty once claimed that irony was the key to understanding history. Indeed, irony may be the key to understanding the human condition.

There are plenty of songs about a man feeling bad over a woman who has done him wrong. Consider the piercing lyric from "Grievin' Me Blues": "I'm so sad and lonely, love has been refused." When Dorsey wrote these types of songs for Ma Rainey, the man was the culprit. In Ma Rainey's "Last Minute Blues," released by Paramount in 1923, Dorsey's abilities as a songwriter shine through the dreary mood of the lyric, "Minutes seem like hours, hours seem like days/ It seems like my daddy won't stop his evil ways. . . . The brook runs into the river, river runs into the sea/If I don't run into daddy, somebody'll have to bury me." His humor also punches the last line, "If anybody asks you, who wrote this lonesome song/Tell them you don't know the writer, but Ma Rainey put it on."

Dorsey also knew a thing or two about poverty and suffering. In "Broke Man's Blues," he bemoans, "I'm feeling like an outcast, looking like a tramp/Can't price a postcard, can't even buy a stamp." But one of those "moanin' blues" songs where the spirituals broke in comes in a song recorded in 1930 in Richmond, Indiana, for the smaller label Gennett. "Maybe It's the Blues" picks up the same angst that would come to plague Muddy Waters a decade later in his recording of "I Be's Troubled." The first lines hammer the theme, "Something pounding in my breast/When I lay down to take my rest/Horrid nightmares, scary dreams/Then the blues steps on the scene." He steps back for some perspective, "Maybe it's the blues that keeps me worried all the time," before in vain frustration exclaiming, "If only I could lose these weary blues that's on my mind." Sounding like an old man with a lot of regrets, he laments the "happiness that comes around, but never comes to stay." Again in frustration, he pleads, "If I only had someone just to drive my tears away." The song ends on this note of desolation. Dorsey filled "Take My Hand, Precious Lord" with the same levels of angst, only in this latter song, he manages to find resolution. And that resolution was christological.

The birth of Christ struck a chord with the African American experience that reverberated through the spirituals. I readily remember as a white, suburban kid singing "Go

Tell It on the Mountain" in summer camps, Sunday schools, and church meetings. But, as James Cone points out, the event of Jesus's birth was far eclipsed in the spirituals by his life, which was in turn eclipsed by his death, which was in turn eclipsed by his resurrection. More often than not, it's the victorious Jesus, the one who has conquered death and stands on the other side of Jordan's shores, who meets us in the spirituals. Yet the victorious Jesus meets us precisely because he met with us in his life and at the cross. The life, death, and resurrection of Christ become, in the estimation of Cone, the "particular focal points of the spirituals." In his life, Jesus was the oppressed one who always raised a hand for the downtrodden. In his death, he not only identified fully with suffering, but thereby purchased freedom and redemption. In his resurrection, he conquers death and promises new life in heaven, standing on that other shore. All these themes overflow the spirituals. Jesus's life, death, and resurrection also find their way into the blues. It is also in the life, death, and resurrection of Jesus that we see what it means to be fully human.[9]

The blues, as the previous chapters have revealed, have provided insight into the rich textures of the human condition. The blues forces those who might otherwise prefer to look away to look upon Adam and Eve as God hands down the curse upon them. The blues forces us to embrace our identity in Adam, to embrace our fallenness and our limitations, and also to embrace the fallenness and the limitations of the world in which we live. But being in Adam only partly defines the human condition, and the curse holds but a conditional and temporary restraining order on the world. Paul fills in the picture for us by looking to Christ. He defines Christ as the final Adam. (The literal meaning of the Greek word that Paul uses is that Christ is the eschatological Adam [1 Cor. 15:45].) The blues forces us to embrace our identity in Adam, to be sure. But if we listen closely enough, the blues will force us to embrace Christ also.

When Jesus Wept: Embracing the Curse

The first rhythms of Jesus that we hear sound remarkably similar to those of Adam. Though sinless, Jesus endured all the hardship and limitations of life in a fallen world. Contrary to the well-worn Victorian hymn, we may well assume that as an infant he cried. We know for certain that as an adult he did. The progenitor of choral music in America, the colonial figure William Billings, seized hold of that moment in the Gospels when Jesus stood weeping at the grave of Lazarus (John 11):

> When Jesus wept, a falling tear
> In mercy flowed beyond all bound.
> When Jesus groaned, a trembling fear
> Seized all the guilty world around.

That wasn't the only time Jesus wept; he wept over Jerusalem and he wept in utter agony in the Garden of Gethsemane. Neither was that the only Lazarus in the Gospels. The other Lazarus, contrasted with the rich man, also captured attention (Luke 16). Poor, or Po', Lazarus was but one of a cast of many of the poor and needy. But his was also a special case. Justice prevailed. Lazarus was exalted; the rich man, who came to be called Mr. Dives in the spirituals, was punished. This socially subversive narrative boomed through the spirituals:

> Poor man Lazarus, poor as I, don't you see?
> Poor man Lazarus, poor as I,
> When he died, he foun' a home on high . . .
>
> Rich man, Dives, he lived so well, don't you see?
> Rich man, Dives, he lived so well,
> When he died he found a home in Hell.

We shouldn't miss the way the song connects with Lazarus, evidenced in exclaiming "poor as I." This movement between the singer and the gospel character, though gapped by nearly two millennia, occurred fluidly and freely in the spirituals. When singing about the "Blind man lyin' at the pool," the pronouns are not "his" or "him," but "my" and "me." So the lyric runs, "Lord, remember me" and "Lord, save me." The poor, the blind, the lame, they all met Jesus, finding him sympathetic. It was the woman who suffered from a type of hemorrhaging who just reached out to touch a piece of Jesus's garment that so struck Blind Willie Johnson in his song "I Know His Blood Can Make Me Whole."[10]

These characters in the Gospels knew hardship, as did the blues singers. These characters also tended to find the resolution to their troubles outside of the parameters of the religious establishment, as did the blues singers. James "Kokomo" Arnold, like Georgia Tom Dorsey, left Georgia for a career in Chicago. His first career wasn't blues, however. He was a bootlegger who played slide guitar on the side. He made his first recordings in Memphis in 1930. Back in Chicago, he continued to record, including "Mean Old Twister Blues," for Decca in 1937. In this song he makes a jab at the religious establishment. There's a twister coming, "poor people runnin' every which a-way." He intones, "Everybody's got to wonder, what's the matter with this cruel world today?" In effect this song raises the question that has plagued philosophers since Plato wrestled with it in his dialogue "Euthyphro." This blues song raises the question of theodicy, the conundrum of a good and powerful and just God on the one hand, and a world filled with evil and sorrow on the other. For "Kokomo" James, this was no mere philosophical question. This was an urgent, existential one. The question "What is the matter with this world?" arises from the depths of his soul, not from the musings of the academy. Once Arnold asks the question, he entertains the pat answer handed down by the religious establishment:

> Now my mama told me, when I was only five months
>   old:
> If you obey your preacher, the good Lord is going to
>   bless your soul.

While this formulaic approach might have worked for him
as a child, it showed fault lines as he got older:

> Now the daylight is failing, and the moon begin to
>   rise.
> I'm just down here weeping and moaning, right by
>   my mama's side.[11]

Arnold was having difficulty bringing together what he
had been taught in the church with what he was seeing in
the world. Bluesman Francis "Scrapper" Blackwell can sym-
pathize. In his "Trouble Blues," recorded in Chicago in 1928,
he moans, "I wonder why trouble keeps on worrying me/I'd
just soon have my body, baby, buried in the sea." In his "Dry
Spell Blues," Son House can't even speak of his troubles, but
merely surrenders to them: "I done throwed up my hands,
Lord." Maggie Jones, who toured alongside of Ma Rainey
and Bessie Smith throughout the 1920s, also exhausts her
attempts to live in this cruel world. In "Suicide Blues" she
confesses, "I was tired of living," before offering a farewell:
"So goodbye old cold world, I'm glad you're left behind." To
this short list could be added many others.

These blues singers, all well versed in the church, found
the answers in that church to not be compelling in light of
what they experienced in the world. They turned to the blues
to try to find some answers. The blues helped them ask the
questions. The blues gave voice to those questions and gave
voice to those sorrows from which the questions sprang.
But the blues didn't always answer those questions, either.
Walter Vinson, from the town of Bolton, just outside Jackson,
Mississippi, reveals how these questions went unanswered

in just three little words from his 1930 recording "Unhappy Blues." He weeps, "I'm so unhappy."

The types of hardships faced by the blues singers might have differed in some respects from the hardships endured by those in the pages of the gospel narratives. The gospel characters didn't have to face the boll weevil or the floodwaters of the Mississippi River. But in many respects, the hardships of these two groups separated by continents and by centuries are remarkably identical. And the people of the Gospels, like the blues singers, found themselves turned out from the religious establishment of their day. The blind weren't met with compassion but were instead the object of philosophical debate. Whose sin caused this, the religious leaders bickered, his mother's or his father's? Jesus cut this knot at its very core. He simply healed the man. As the life of Jesus unfolds in the pages of the Gospels, compassion extends to such as these—the poor, the blind, those caught in the clutches of their own sin—a compassion that extends to the likes of Son House, "Kokomo" Arnold, "Scrapper" Blackwell, Maggie Jones, and Walter Vinson.

The word *compassion* is a synonym for *sympathy*. Jesus not only extends compassion to the outcast, but also suffers with the outcast. That *suffering with* reached a climax as his earthly life came to an end on a cross at Calvary. Jesus did not merely look upon the sin-cursed world from afar. Jesus entered the world of Adam and Eve, the cursed world of the cursed. Before he conquered that curse, he embraced it. He endured it. He wept as he felt its effect.

Why Have You Forsaken Me? Embracing the Cross

Being alone is nearly a prerequisite for a blues singer. It's not, "I'm surrounded by my friends, I have my family, I have my woman." Instead, it's "I'm alone," and everyone—friends, family, and even the best woman—has left me. The first blues song, if one credits W. C. Handy with the discovery of the blues, is his "St. Louis Blues." It was indeed the first published song with the word *blues* in the title. The song sounds a bit too ragtime to be considered alongside of the true Delta blues, but the lyric warrants a hearing:

> I hate to see that evening sun go down,
> I hate to see that evening sun go down,
> 'Cause, my baby, she's done left this town.
> Feelin' tomorrow like I feel today,
> If I'm feelin' tomorrow like I feel today,
> I'll pack my trunk and make my get-away.

The line "Feelin' tomorrow like I feel today" gets a lot of mileage in the blues. Muddy Waters incorporated it in "I Be's Troubled," later recorded as "Can't Be Satisfied." The first verse too became well traveled. In fact, it's fitting that this is the first blues recording, since it's essentially the blues compacted in one song. There's subversion. The evening sun is supposed to bring relief. It signals the end of the workday, a time of rest. But in this song it brings grief. It calls forth the night, darkness. There's that staple of the blues, a woman who has done her man wrong (unless Bessie Smith is singing the song, and then it's a man who's to blame). There's also the restlessness, the rambling. And this restlessness is triggered by one fact: the singer is alone, alone to face the night.

Mississippi John Hurt wore his loneliness as a heavy burden. He recorded some great blues in the 1920s, then disappeared until his rediscovery in the early 1960s, just before his death on November 2, 1966. He, of course, didn't actually disappear. He was living in Avalon, Mississippi, the entire time. He even left those who wanted to find him a rather obvious clue. One of those 1920s blues of his is entitled "Avalon Blues." All anyone had to do to find him was listen to the music. It also pays to listen to another of his 1920s blues, "Blue Harvest Blues," another song of subversion.

Harvest time is supposed to be a time of joy, a time of plenty. Not in this song. Hurt's put all his money into the crop. He had to buy his seeds, feed his mules, and pay the plantation owner his rent for the privilege of plowing and sowing those fields. And this year it looks like a bad harvest. He might, however, be able to bear through yet another bad crop. But, as the song reaches the end, what really troubles him is that he's alone:

> Ain't got no mother, father left me long ago
> I'm just like an orphan, where my folks is I don't
>   know
> Blues around my shoulder, blues are all around my
>   head
> With my heavy burden, Lord, I wished I was dead.

The level of desolation in this song is matched in the spiritual "Sometimes I Feel like a Motherless Child," the same spiritual from which Blind Willie Johnson borrowed lines for his blues song "Mother's Children Have a Hard Time."

> Sometimes I feel like a motherless child,
> Sometimes I feel like a motherless child,
> Sometimes I feel like a motherless child,
> A long ways from home, a long ways from home.
> Sometimes I feel like I'm almost gone,
> Sometimes I feel like I'm almost gone,
> Sometimes I feel like I'm almost gone,
> A long ways from home, a long ways from home.
> Oh Believer.
> A long ways from home, a long ways from home.

On the cross, Jesus was not merely a long ways from home. The incarnation and his life on earth accomplished that much. On the cross, Christ was nowhere. On the cross, Christ was fatherless, abandoned by God. Writer and social critic Stanley Crouch has referred to Christ's exclamation of dereliction, "My God, my God, why have you forsaken me," as "the greatest blues line of all time." And on the cross, as darkness covered the face of the earth, Jesus entered the dark night of his soul alone.[12]

This loneliness leaves one with little to say. Ed Bell, a bluesman from Alabama, made his recordings on the Columbia label in the late 1920s and 1930. The wake of the Great Depression that ended that decade forced Bell to sell his guitar and leave the blues. Though he lived until the 1960s, unlike Mississippi John Hurt he never even got rediscovered. One of his last blues, "Bad Boy," chronicles the loss of hope of one cast in prison. Somewhat prophetically, the last line concedes, "I ain't going to sing no more, baby that is all." Not singing anymore is tantamount to giving up altogether. The narrator in that song had reached a point of having nothing more to say. We meet the same silence in the spiritual "I Couldn't Hear Nobody Pray." The narrator is again alone, "way down yonder by myself." But here praying is given up instead of singing. Hope falls prey to loneliness. And in that loneliness there is only silence. As the song unfolds, the loneliness encroaches until it engulfs: "In the valley," silence; "On my knees," silence; "With my burden," silence. Only at the end do the loneliness and the silence break. An ecstatic "Hallelujah!" finally shatters the silence as the narrator roars, "Trouble's over," as he finds himself "in the kingdom with Jesus."

This loneliness experienced in the blues and spirituals harbors fears of death. The "coolin' board," on which dead bodies were laid during plans for funeral and burial, ranks as one of the most dismal images in the blues. In Son House's "Death Letter Blues," by the time he makes it to the hospital, the woman he loved is already "on the coolin' board." Blind Willie McTell even named a song after it, "Coolin' Board Blues."

There are conflicting stories regarding Blind Willie McTell. Some of them have him blind at birth, while others have him losing his sight in his teens. While McTell recorded consistently from the 1920s through the 1950s, his music received the most attention when the Allman Brothers adopted his "Statesboro Blues" as their own in the late 1960s. In "Talking to Myself," McTell pleads, "Good Lord, good Lord, send me an angel down." God (presumably) replies, "Can't spare you no angel, but I'll swear I'll send you a teasing brown." And, as any listener of the blues can guess, that woman turned bad. As in the rest of the blues, McTell's women are reckless (for example, "Stomp Down Rider") and crooked (as in "Southern Can Is Mine"). In general, Blind Willie McTell testifies they "mean me no good at all," a lyric appearing in a number of his songs. Despite this unrequited love and ill treatment, McTell hopelessly clings to love:

> I went down to my praying ground, and fell on
> bended knees,
> I ain't cryin' for no religion, Lordy give me back my
> good gal please.

Whether or not that prayer, from "Broke Down Engine Blues," was answered didn't stop McTell from uttering another prayer, this time in a more dire circumstance, in his "Coolin' Board Blues." "Don't a man feel bad, when his baby's on the coolin' board/Don't a man feel bad, when the hearse pulls up to his door," McTell begins his moanin' blues. He pleads, "Undertaker, undertaker, don't drive so fast/seem like every minute going to be my last." By the time he makes it to the end of the song, McTell poignantly expresses the pain of death:

> When I walked up to her bedside, her breath was get-
> tin' low
> She looked at me and said, "Honey, I can't love you
> no more"
> My heart struck sorrow, my tears falling down,
> watching my baby settled into the ground.

The loneliness in the blues isn't only owing to mistreating men and women; it also is owing to death. Even in a wash of soured relationships, the separation of death becomes too much to bear. The blues neither glorifies nor sentimentalizes death. Neither does the blues sidestep or avoid death. In its clear-eyed acceptance of the curse, the blues treats death as the reality that it indeed is, the ugly reality that it is. So too do the spirituals.

McTell's death blues borrows phrases from one of the more well-traveled spirituals that engages the issue of death, "Will the Circle Be Unbroken?" Though almost inextricably linked with the Carter family, the musical family Johnny Cash married into, this song has a curious history in American folk music that predates Tennessee's beloved musical family. It was written by Ada Habersham in Britain in 1907. Her hymns and spirituals traveled to America with Dwight L. Moody and his songman Ira Sankey after one of their many campaigns across the Atlantic. The Carter Family produced the song under their own arrangement, making it a staple in the southern folk circuit. In the Carter Family version the hearse is coming to take away the narrator's mother. Here the plea to the undertaker is, "Undertaker please drive slow/For this body you are hauling, Lord, I hate to see her go." With any determination that can be mustered, the narrator vows, "I will try to hold up and be brave." But to no avail. "I could not hold my sorrow," comes the admission, "when they laid her in the grave." The chorus asks the rhetorical question, "Will the circle be unbroken?" The answer comes in the response, "There's a better home awaiting/In the sky, Lord, in the sky."

Pops Staples of the Staple Singers, the musical "first family" of the civil rights movement, made, hands-down, the best recording of this song. And that recording made this song one of the many anthems of the civil rights movement. Pops's gentle voice barely lifts the lyric over the music. His performance comes from deep within. The song does not flinch from the harsh reality of the limits of life, the limits inherent in the human condition. Death has a way of showing us where those limits lie. Emily Dickinson playfully, but with the precision of a surgeon's knife, muses, "Because I could not stop for Death/He kindly stopped for me." Life in the twenty-first century, given the increasing technologizing of the world, is much more adamant in its refusal to stop for death. Life in the twenty-first century is eerily hell-bent on avoiding the curse handed down in the Garden of Eden, the curse that introduced death and decay into the very heart of verdant life. But the unavoidable is truly unavoidable, after all. "I am carryed towards the West," John Donne vainly declares, before conceding, "when my Soules forme bends towards the East." That ever-moving-forward optimism of the modern and postmodern eras is indeed kept in check by our own limitations. It is kept in check by the curse.[13]

Death mercilessly stops for us. In the words of blues singer the reverend Blind Gary Davis, "Death don't have no mercy. . . . Death will leave you standin' and cryin' in this land." Jesus did not overcome death by avoiding it. He did not overcome death by merely elongating life expectancy. He overcame death by dying. He overcame the curse by meeting it head on.[14]

In chapter 3 I referred to the movie *O Brother, Where Art Thou?* Its runaway success likely had something to do with the soundtrack. Music plays a comic role in that movie and, like soundtracks are supposed to, it moves the narrative along. But the most powerful role music plays in that movie is setting the dark scenes of the film. Ralph Stanley's haunting a cappella rendition of "O Death" drives a somber cloud over this already dark comedy by the Coen brothers. And then there's the scene of the hanging of George Clooney's character, Ulysses Everett McGill, once the law finally catches up with him. The gravediggers, played by the Fairfield Four, help him prepare for death by singing the old spiritual "You've Got to Walk That Lonesome Valley," also known simply as "That Lonesome Valley." Like "Will the Circle Be Unbroken?" this spiritual sees death and the loneliness that descends because of it with a clear-eyed realism sometimes missing in our current attitudes toward death. In "Will the Circle," the loneliness descends upon those left behind. In "That Lonesome Valley," the loneliness overruns the one who faces death.

"You've got to go through the lonesome valley/You got to go there yourself," the song howls. "You've got to go cross the River Jordan by yourself . . . You've got to face it for yourself." The song is relentless in its assault upon the soul. "No one here can go with you." But the song is only partially true. Death is a solitary journey. There is one, however, who has gone on before. The eschatological human, Jesus, has gone through death. He is not doomed by death as the first man and woman were, but he is the one through whom death is swallowed up (1 Cor. 15:54). He has gone through that valley, and he casts a sheltering presence over those who come through it after him.

It is the cross that both answers for the curse and speaks to the curse. It answers for the curse by enduring death, limits, frailty, weakness, and, ultimately, the wrath of God, symbolized in the cup that runs over. It speaks to the curse by completing the picture of what it means to be human. We are human when we realize our identity in Adam, when we embrace the curse and accept our limitations and our frailty and our weaknesses. We are human when we realize our identity in Christ, when we embrace the cross and accept again our own limitations. It was Martin Luther who wonderfully put it, that the cross is "God's no" to human achievement. While the cross is God's no to us on one level, on another it is God's yes to us. God said yes to us in creation, even though Adam and Eve said no. When Adam and Eve said no, they rejected the limitation God had put upon them. They became seduced by the promise to become like God, to surpass their status as creature and to rival the creator. Ironically, the curse, their penalty, only steeped them deeper in their creatureliness and distanced them further from their creator. Despite humanity's no to God, he again said yes to us in the cross. Jesus endured God's no when he cried, "My God, My God, why have you forsaken me?" We are truly human when we embrace both the curse and the cross, when we turn our no into yes.[15]

The spirituals turned their no into yes by trying to keep watch with Christ in Gethsemane. In fact, they went one step further, trying to keep watch with Christ at Calvary. "Were you there," the spiritual asks, "when they crucified my Lord?" The reverend Blind Gary Davis, who migrated from the red-clay soils of the Piedmont in South Carolina to the streets of Harlem, where he was named the blues-playing preacher, balked at identifying with Christ in his song "Crucifixion." Instead, Davis, through the voice of the song's narrator, identifies with the people who were there. Davis identifies with Peter brazenly declaring that he will not betray his master. In a chilling verse, Davis draws us in to identify with the soldiers who "smoted my Lord across the head with reed" and who thrust a crown of thorns upon his head. The last person to whom Davis connects the listener is Pilate, who calls out, "Bring me a basin of water to wash my hands." Vainly, Pilate bellows, "I don't want to be guilty of an innocent man." Each verse thunders a resounding no to Christ, whether that no comes from the lips of Roman soldiers or from bureaucrats, or even from the lips of a trusted follower. The reverend Blind Gary Davis uses the events of the crucifixion to show why there had to be a crucifixion. Christ died, was compelled to die, because we say no. Only through his death may our no become yes.

He Rose from the Dead: Embracing the Resurrection

Allowing Jesus to fully define what it means to be human encompasses not only his life and his death, but also his resurrection. Through his resurrection we become not only what God intended for us to become in the Garden of Eden, but, in the words of Paul, much more (Rom. 5). We become true image bearers.

Blind Lemon Jefferson enjoyed recording spirituals, upon which he would put his unmistakable mark. One such song was "He Arose from the Dead." Sonorous and smooth, Jefferson patiently recalls the details of resurrection morning: the angels come to roll away the stone, the disciples are instructed that Christ has arisen. Blind Lemon Jefferson even includes Christ's post-resurrection instruction to Peter, "Feed my lambs" (John 21:15 KJV). The main theme of the song, repeated again and again, concerns that which the resurrection accomplishes. This comes through in the final line of the chorus:

> He rose, he rose, he rose from the dead
> He rose, he rose, he rose from the dead
> He rose, he rose, he rose from the dead
> And the Lord shall bear my spirit home.

Christ's resurrection makes possible the resurrection of Adam's fallen race—Blind Lemon Jefferson and us included. At the cross, Christ's obedience to the Father undoes Adam and Eve's act of disobedience. It is his yes against their no. At the resurrection, Christ does what Adam could never do. In his resurrection, in the words of James Cone, Jesus "put an end to human bondage."[16]

Christ surpasses not only Adam, but also, as the biblical story unfolds, Moses, the great liberator in the pages of the Old Testament. This is what Cone's understanding of the resurrection alludes to. The New Testament event of the resurrection became conflated with the Old Testament event of the exodus. And the spirituals were replete with references to this motif.

Crossing through the river or through the "lonesome valley" as a metaphor for death, which occurs throughout the spirituals, has a lot less to do with Greek mythology and the River Styx than with the exodus motif. There's a simple cosmology that dominates African American spirituals and the religious consciousness and theology that those spirituals fostered. There's Egypt, the place of bondage for them both as slaves and even in the post-Reconstruction South. There's the exodus, sometimes symbolized in the spirituals as the crossing of the Red Sea, and most times as the crossing of the Jordan River. Either symbol chiefly represents death, though in slavery times these symbols also represented freedom through the Underground Railroad. Finally, there's the Promised Land. This latter one looks on the surface to be heaven, but peering beneath the surface, one finds the hope that some, even just a bit, of that heaven would break through to life on earth. This fundamentally differs from the early non–African American religious cosmology, informed as it is by Puritan sensibilities. The Puritans dubbed the Old World as Egypt, the crossing of the Atlantic as the exodus, and the New World as the Promised Land, as Zion, "the City upon a hill." Allan Dwight Callahan cleverly highlights the difference in these cosmologies: "The land that the puritan founders called the Promised Land has been Pharaoh's Egypt for African Americans."[17] A distinct reading of the text and particular appropriations of the text will likely follow from such disparate cosmologies.

This distinct appropriation of texts is best seen in the spiritual "Oh Mary, Don't You Weep." The Mary in this spiritual is most likely the sister of Lazarus, the Lazarus from John 11. "Oh Mary, don't you weep, don't you mourn," picks up on Mary's sadness over Lazarus's death (John 11:33). But then the song takes a decidedly odd turn. The very next line, the reason why Mary is not to weep is, "Pharoah's army got drowned." This song conflates centuries in a mere flash. Bruno Chenu in his study of the spirituals explains why: "This spiritual links the Christ of the resurrection to the God of the Exodus." Mary need not weep because the new Moses has brought about a new exodus, with the promise of new life to come. Israel will not be abandoned in the land of Egypt as Pharaoh's slaves but will instead be brought into freedom. So too we will not be abandoned at death, but will be brought forth into new life. Again, James Cone explains, "The cross was not the end of God's drama of salvation. Death does not have the last word." The exodus and the resurrection are both freedom from bondage, slavery in the one case and sin in the other. The spiritual reads these events seamlessly.[18]

What is even more remarkable in the lyrics of this particular spiritual is the way Christ fills it without even being mentioned within its lyrics. This again speaks to the way that biblical texts are read and appropriated within this African American cosmology and worldview. Christ inhabits this worldview so fully and palpably that he need not even be mentioned. This is the Christ-haunted South from which these spirituals came into being. He is always there. The place where Christ may be found most often in these spirituals is on the other side of Jordan's shores, standing with welcoming arms outstretched. He can stand on the shore with integrity, because he walked on the other side, in Pharaoh's Egypt. And he passed through the sea.

One more thing can be said of the resurrection and the human condition. Once again, James Cone: "For black slaves, Jesus is God breaking into their historical present and transforming it according to divine expectations." In the abhorrent, nearly unimaginable historical present of black slaves in America, the divine expectation of liberation from bondage surely meant a great deal—perhaps a great deal more than it can mean to most others living in a different historical present. But no matter what historical present one happens to be in, the divine expectation is the only mechanism, the only means by which anyone can make sense of the world and find hope. It is ultimately the resurrection that speaks to the human condition.[19]

Admittedly, the blues makes little reference to the resurrection, except when singers wished for possession over judgment day. Robert Johnson would use his powers to get even with all of those women who had done him wrong. Muddy Waters would be more magnanimous; he would use his powers to reward his women, all of them. The absence of the resurrection in the blues is rather disconcerting, for the resurrection is ultimately the means of hope. The historical present surely abides in the blues. Worrying, rambling, wandering, crying, moaning flow from song to song to song. These are instances of a historical present that yearns for divine expectation. Again, it is ultimately the resurrection that speaks to the human condition. Sometimes, emphases on the resurrection amount to nothing more than escapism. The resurrection as a way out can be used to shirk responsibilities, to ignore making a difference here, in this life. The blues certainly does not suffer from such escapism. Blues errs in the other direction, which is tragic. The resurrection is not a means of escape but the only means of hope.

The blues is also Christ-haunted, though not entirely in the same way as the spirituals. In the latter, Jesus, while not always mentioned, is known to be there, the buoy in the time of storm. In the blues, Jesus could be the buoy in the time of storm, and the one who would take burdens away. He could be the one who would bring divine expectation into the historical present. Sometimes that Christ-haunted nature of the blues lies deep beneath the surface, which is to say, sometimes it's hard to find it. But at other times, that which is Christ-haunted becomes rather transparently Christ-present.

Though he was born and made his home in Rossville, Tennessee, just on the other side of the border, Fred McDowell garnered the name Mississippi Fred McDowell. "I seem like I'm at home when I'm there in Mississippi," he said. He should have, for he cut his musical teeth in the Delta. Alan Lomax called McDowell, born in 1904, "quite the equal of Son House and Muddy Waters." Praise from Caesar is praise indeed. McDowell was a farmer. "And whenever you get somebody, you know, you want to plow for you," he once said, "you just call for Fred McDowell." You might have done better, though, to call him if you needed a singer. He learned to play slide guitar with a beef bone before trading up to a bottleneck. One of the songs he played with that bottleneck guitar, adding his rough-hewn vocals, was "Glory, Glory, Hallelujah," longing for the day "over yonder" when he would lay his burden down, when he would go home to be with Jesus. That's for the life to come. In this life, McDowell also turns to Jesus in "Jesus Is on the Mainline." Since "Jesus is on the mainline," McDowell says simply, "call him up and tell him . . . if you are in trouble . . . if you are sick." McDowell introduces this song with a spoken line: "Jesus man is on the mainline." The song also personalizes the plea. Jesus becomes "my Jesus," who will come in a hurry. McDowell feels at ease in this song, without the strained vocals that pepper most of his other songs. His ease stems from the confidence he has in the one of whom he sings. Jesus is on the mainline because he entered this life, entering into our troubles and our sorrow. He is also on the mainline through the power of the resurrection.[20]

I Want to Be like Jesus in My Heart

Blind Lemon Jefferson offers an earnest prayer in his song "I Want to Be like Jesus in My Heart," his version of the spiritual "I Want to Be a Christian." As Blind Lemon Jefferson's voice rises over his strumming of a banjo, which replaced his guitar for this particular recording, one can almost hear the remembrances of past failures alongside expectations of future ones. Blind Lemon Jefferson may very well be banking on sincerity in the place of his moral will. His version of this old spiritual has five verses, consisting of, essentially, four simple lines, the last verse repeating the first:

Lord I so want to be like Jesus in my heart, in my
heart.
Lord I so want to be like Jesus in my heart.
In my heart, in my heart, in my heart, in my heart.
Lord I so want to be like Jesus in my heart.
Lord, I want to cross the River of Jordan in my heart,
in my heart.

Lord I don't want to be a liar in my heart, in my
heart.

Lord I want to love my neighbor in my heart, in my
heart.

Lord I so want to be like Jesus in my heart, in my
heart.

Unlike Thomas Dorsey, who battled with his two personas, Blind Lemon Jefferson moved freely between his two. As mentioned in the previous chapter, Blind Lemon Jefferson's persona for the spirituals was the pseudonym Deacon L. J. Bates. He alternately recorded as both. He seems to have adopted these two personas for commercial reasons. Church-going folks would have a hard time buying their religious 78s by the same guy who sang "Black Snake Moan," even though most of these record buyers likely had both in their record cabinets. That's not to say that Blind Lemon Jefferson didn't have his internal struggles. Can't we all sing with him, "Lord, I want to be like Jesus in my heart"? He voices that frustration of all those who know full well their identity in Adam and Eve and are striving to understand their new identity in Christ.

In the incarnation, Christ identified with all the sons of Adam and all the daughters of Eve. He came as an infant, embracing the curse of the human condition. He is not aloof, not far off. Thomas A. Dorsey could plead, "I am tired, I am weak, I am worn," before the feet of one who, too, was tired, weak, and worn. He could plead "when the darkness appears" to one who not only experienced darkness, but experienced a darkness greater than that endured by any other human being.

Mount Zion Missionary Baptist Church, Morgan City, Mississippi (pop. 300), one of four burial sites for Robert Johnson. This one has the monument by Columbia Records.

6

Come Sunday

Living in This World, Longing for the Next

A Christian is obligated to certain things.

Rubin Lacy

Through all the sorrow songs there breathes a
hope—a faith in the ultimate justice of things. . . .
Sometimes it is a faith in life, sometimes a faith in
death.

W. E. B. Du Bois

Historians of the blues look to Muddy Waters as the
link from the rough and raw sound of the Delta
blues to the electrified urban blues to the megabusiness of rock. When Muddy Waters went north in 1943, he
took with him that sound, the slide guitar and the moaning
vocals. He was the trustee of a sound that stretched back in

time to Son House, Robert Johnson, and Charley Patton, a sound that would push forward in time to 1960s rockers on both sides of the Atlantic. He was also the trustee of a lyric, "I got the blues, can't be satisfied." That lyric also stretched back in time, past House, Johnson, and Patton. It stretched back to groups huddled in the woods circled around a fire or gathered around tables in plantation shacks. When Muddy Waters took that sound and that lyric with him and crossed a line stretched out across America on the 39th parallel, he could do so without the fear of being chased by bounty hunters. Some of that lyric also stretched forward. Steve Turner's *Hungry for Heaven: Rock 'n' Roll & the Search for Redemption* shows how one should not write off this pop music form of rock 'n' roll as uninterested in profound questions, or even religious questions. Yet some of that lyric that Muddy Waters brought along with him did slip away. The deep, soul-wrenching angst of Waters's lyrics became trivialized to the degree that sharecroppers' lives can be compared to those of suburban teenagers. Some things get lost in translation.

Nevertheless, Muddy Waters is indeed a link. But he's not the only link. There were other Mississippi musicians who also made the trek, taking the sound and the lyric with them. It may seem remarkable that in a book on the blues only passing reference has been made to the legendary B. B. [the] King, but this chapter remedies that. Here too we meet another musician, one not as famous but as crucial, especially in terms of that precious commodity that was taken north—the lyric. J. B. Lenoir, unlike King, did not hail from the Mississippi Delta. He lived along another river snaking its way through the Magnolia State, the Pearl River. Growing up in Monticello, south of Jackson and closer to the gulf than to the Delta, Lenoir first headed to New Orleans before taking the train north to Chicago. Muddy Waters, B. B. King, J. B. Lenoir, and many others went north looking for something more, "rolling stones" who weren't satisfied. But in the end, their legends were not carved out of that which they were seeking, but rather out of that which they brought with them. Their legends came from the lyric, cultivated and nurtured like the crops rooted in that deep, black, fertile soil of Mississippi's river bottoms.

Obligations

"Rube" Lacy, the bluesman—or Rev. Rubin Lacy, the preacher—once said of the blues, "Sometimes the best Christian in the world have the blues quicker than a sinner do." He explains, "The average sinner ain't got nothin' to worry about. He do what he please, go where he please, use what he please." But not so, reasons Lacy, for the Christian, "But a Christian is obligated to certain things and obligated not to do certain things. That sometimes cause the Christian to take the blues." Lacy chose the pulpit over the juke joint in his effort to come to terms with those obligations, to come to terms with the blues. J. B. Lenoir chose the juke joint. But Lenoir knew some things about obligations. He defined the blues similarly to Rube Lacy as a worried and troubled mind: "The blues is sprung up from troubles and heartaches, being bound and down." Lenoir also ups the ante: "The blues is originated from the blackman's headaches and his troubles. And he have a lot of it."[1]

Both of Lenoir's parents played the guitar and played the blues, for a time that is. In Paul Oliver's *Conversations with the Blues*, Lenoir recalls what made his father give it up. One night his father had a dream, a nightmare, in which he was chased by the devil himself. Rather than make the deal for his soul, Lenoir's father left the blues and turned to preaching. Later, for a time, so did his son. J. B. Lenoir was born on March 5, 1929, when blues was already in full swing and race records filled the shelves at the general stores. The preaching didn't last long for Lenoir, for by the 1940s he was already playing at picnics and fish fries. By the mid-1940s he ended up in

New Orleans, teaming up with fellow Mississippi transplants Elmore James and Sonny Boy Williamson #2.[2] By 1949, he was on to Chicago, recording throughout the 1950s. In the 1960s he enjoyed his success, touring the United States and Europe. In 1967, after suffering a heart attack as a result of a car accident, J. B. Lenoir died in Urbana, Illinois, a little over a hundred miles from Chicago. His body was returned to Monticello, Mississippi, buried next to that of his wife, Ella L. Craft. The gravestone's inscription reads, "Let the works we've done speak for us." The musical works of his life, while having their roots in Mississippi, were fostered along by that community of transplanted musicians in New Orleans: Lenoir, Elmore James, and Sonny Boy Williamson #2.[3]

Elmore James was born Elmore Brooks in Richland, Mississippi, just outside of Jackson. When he was a child, his family moved into the Delta, to the town of Belzoni, to work as sharecroppers. James gave up sharecropping for the guitar. His timing couldn't have been better. He was able to hear Charley Patton, now near the end of his life, who often traveled the short distance from his home base in Holly Ridge to the town of Belzoni. He also met up with Robert Johnson in 1937, just one year before Johnson's death. Though the encounter was brief, Robert Santelli reveals Johnson's impact: "He left an indelible mark on James, who made Johnson's slide guitar technique the most important element in his own style." Santelli also notes how his "reinvention" of Johnson's "I Believe I'll Dust My Broom" catapulted James onto the blues scene. One final influence came through Sonny Boy Williamson #2, who in the late 1930s was living in Belzoni in a run-down shack. James teamed up with this harmonica player, born Rice Miller, or Aleck Miller, but known by his performance name, Sonny Boy Williamson #2. He wasn't, however, merely a harmonica player. He and Sonny Boy Williamson #1 vie for the position of the greatest harmonica player of the blues. Together they are hailed as the architects of blues harmonica,

"A Blues for Duke Ellington"

I was waitin' on a dream, waitin' through the
    night.
I was waitin' on a dream, waitin' through the
    night.
Just speak a word, speak a word and I'll come
    to life.

SJN

credited with transforming the harmonica from a sort of novelty instrument in jug bands.[4]

Elmore James on the guitar and Sonny Boy Williamson #2 on the harmonica proved a formidable duo, but James's service in the navy during World War II put them on a two-year hiatus. When James returned, they would eventually head to New Orleans, where they picked up a vocalist who could also play the guitar, J. B. Lenoir. After a brief time together, they went their separate ways. Sonny Boy Williamson #2 made some recordings in Jackson in the 1950s. By the 1960s he was sharing the dais with the likes of Eric Clapton and having a very successful time in the London blues scene. He died in 1965 in Helena, Arkansas, but he was buried on the Mississippi side of the Delta in the town of Tutwiler. The blues had come full circle, as this town once had a train platform upon which W. C. Handy discovered the blues in 1903. Among the murals paying homage to this town's place on the musical map, painted upon brick walls standing less than a football field away from where that train platform once stood, is one depicting that event, with Handy and an unknown musician, as well as one dedicated to Sonny Boy Williamson #2, complete with a map to his gravestone a mile or two away. To get there, travel just out of town, past a row of shotgun-shack-style homes, down the gravel road running through the middle of cotton fields, until the little graveyard by the side of the road comes into view. After walking through knee-high weeds, and—as during my visit—after holding friendly stray dogs at bay, a small clearing becomes visible against a row of trees. In the middle of the clearing is the stone erected in 1980, fifteen years after his death, by Trumpet Records, the recording company from Jackson that gave Williamson his break back in 1950.

When these three Mississippi preachers/sharecroppers-turned-blues-men met up together in New Orleans, each developed his own talent that was both original and unique on the one hand and rooted in and owing to a tradition on the other. James's guitar playing, Williamson's harmonica, and Lenoir's vocals all were both pioneering and imitative in the way a standout pupil honors a master. Lenoir developed a falsetto voice that reflected some of the styles of the best of the early Mississippi moaners but also had a sound all its own. So it is with his lyrics. Lenoir left New Orleans for Chicago in 1949. By 1951 he had a recording contract with Chess Records, the label that gave the world Muddy Waters. He continued to record for Chess, with stints at other labels, throughout the 1950s. This was a time when the first lines of the protest songs that would come to dominate much of the music scene in the 1960s weren't even being imagined, let alone heard. This was the era of doo-wop music and sock hops and the hula hoop—heavy on fun, reflecting the postwar boom and optimism. And into this era, Lenoir released his social criticism through music.

In his social criticism, Lenoir reached back into the tradition of the blues. Amid all that lusty bravado and mourning of love lost that reverberates through the blues, voices clamored from time to time, as chapter 4 pointed out, over certain social conditions in dire need of change. But while

Lenoir reached back, he also entered uncharted territory. In 1954 Lenoir released "Eisenhower Blues." Tried to release it, that is. Robert Santelli explains that this song "was so blunt in its criticism of the newly elected president that the White House allegedly had the record all but banned in 1954. Chess was forced to delete all references to Ike, change the 'incendiary' lyrics, and give it a new title, 'Tax Paying Blues.'" Lenoir had a reputation. In 1951, he had released "Korea Blues," followed up by "I'm in Korea," two songs that foreshadowed the war-protest songs that would appear in the 1960s. And in that decade, Lenoir recorded two songs about the war in Vietnam, both released as "Vietnam."[5]

Lenoir seemed to save his best diatribes, however, for wars closer to home, the war against poverty and the simmering battle for civil rights for Southern blacks, the black men and women who suffered a lot of headache and heartache, troubles and worries—the ones who knew how to sing the blues. In these protest songs, Lenoir was looking for a little justice in this world. He was a blues singer who had obligations.

Apocalypse Now

Despite his efforts to see the connections between the spirituals and the blues, James Cone admits that on the surface there appears a significant difference. Both sing of hope, but each locates that hope in a different place. The spirituals tend to be eschatological in their hope. That is to say, they look for relief, for freedom, for justice, in the future. It would be in the new heavens and the new earth that the injustices of this old earth would be finally set right. Blues is a little less patient. Blues, it seems, looks for an earthly hope. But all of this, as Cone points out, is only on the surface. The truth, he reveals, is that the blues and the spirituals both have room for a hope that is at once eschatological *and* earthly, apocalypse then *and* now. The blues and the spirituals may differ in degree between the eschatological and the earthly. The blues tips the balances toward the here-and-now, while the spirituals tip the balance toward the sweet by-and-by. But they both see hope for a better world to be both now and future.

It's worthwhile to pause over Lenoir's songs. People who get banned in one generation often tend to be better accepted in the next. And people who get banned tend to have something important to say, something that might even verge on the prophetic. In his song "Everybody Wants to Know," Lenoir speaks to the issue of poverty, evidenced in hunger and near famine. He warns, "You rich people listen, you better listen real deep/If we poor get so hungry, we gonna take some food to eat." His lyrics take a much more chilling turn in "Born Dead" when he intones, "Every child born in Mississippi/You know the poor child is born dead." The second verse runs:

> When he came into the world, the doctor spank him,
>   the black baby cry,
> When he came into the world, the doctor spank him,
>   the black baby cry,
> Everybody thought he had a life, and that's why the
>   black baby died.

Lenoir sings against what he sees as an oppressive system, a cruel and vicious downward spiral that he takes to be an assault on human dignity, on humanity itself. Lenoir also sings because the infant can't. Not only can't the baby cry, the baby, as the third verse reveals, doesn't even know that he needs to:

> He will never speak his language, he will never speak
>   his mind,
> Lord, he will never speak his language, the poor baby
>   will never speak his mind
> The poor child will never know in his mind why in
>   the world he's so poor.

"Lord, Lord," he pleads in the fourth verse, "why is it so hard to get ahead?"

Lenoir also speaks for the literal dead who have no voice, in the grisly "Down in Mississippi," a song written just after he heard of a report of the slaying of civil rights advocates in his home state. The first verse recalls his native land through the life of a sharecropper, carrying "that old nine-foot sack" through row after row of cotton. Then comes the second verse:

> They have a hunting season on the rabbit, talkin'
>   'bout the little animal
> Shoot 'im boys, you sure gonna go to jail.
> But the season's always open on men, don't nobody
>   need no badge, you know what I'm talking
>   'bout.

He closes the fourth verse with, "You know I feel just like a lucky man to get away with my life."

He memorializes other civil rights activists killed in another southern state in "Alabama Blues." "I will never go back to Alabama," he starts off; "You know they killed my sister and my brother, and the whole world let those peoples go down there free." Lenoir felt a kinship, a solidarity with these victims. His question runs even deeper than who is my neighbor. He asks who is my brother, my sister. As the song unfolds, Lenoir reveals that "a police officer shot him down," so he responds, "I can't help but to sit down and cry sometime, think about how my poor brother lost his life." His final words:

> Alabama, Alabama, why you want to be so mean,
> You got my people behind a barbwire fence,
> Now you tryin' to take my freedom away from me.

The song is more than a dirge. In the second verse, sounding like the psalmist who cries out, "How long, how long?" Lenoir pleads and begs, "Oh God I wish you would rise up one day/ lead my peoples to the land of peace."

John Perkins's brother was killed by a deputy marshal in Hebron, Mississippi. Clyde Perkins had a Purple Heart for his service in World War II. He was also clubbed by the deputy marshal on a hot August Saturday afternoon in 1964 on Hebron's Main Street, standing outside of the theater. Clyde reached for the club, fearing being hit again. The marshal stepped back, drew, his gun and fired twice into Clyde's stomach at close range. The word that Clyde was shot spread quickly, reaching his brother's ears. John Perkins, sixteen years old at the time, sped off for the town doctor's office, where his brother Clyde laid stretched out on a table with his life slipping from him. They were able to stabilize Clyde, load him into a car, and head for the hospital in Jackson. John Perkins recalls the trip: Clyde lay in the back, "his head in my arms, oozing blood and dying by the inches." They made it to the hospital, but Clyde didn't survive.

In 1970, John Perkins, for his civil rights activities, was arrested, beaten, stomped on, kicked, and, moving in and out of consciousness, nearly lost his life in jail at the hands of deputies and highway patrolmen. He was tortured. And in that same prison cell, he moved from anger and hate to love and forgiveness. Like a prophet, he cried out for the realities of the world to come to become true in this world.

When John Perkins wrote his autobiography, he borrowed a line from a prophet of old for the title, *Let Justice Roll Down*. Amos was a good choice. He too had been a farmer from a small town, raising sheep and tending fruit trees instead of picking cotton, but a farmer just the same. Amos too witnessed injustice at the hands of abusive and oppressive authorities. And he too believed in the day when justice would roll down. In fact, he envisioned a world where the people of God, an oppressed people, would rebuild the ruins of their cities, plant vineyards and drink their wine, and make gardens and eat their fruits. He envisioned a time when they would be literally planted on the land, never to be uprooted again (Amos 9:13–15). Not content to allow that promise to be wholly eschatological, Perkins has devoted his life to seeing a little justice in this world.[6]

J. B. Lenoir might have also been such a prophet like Perkins. A car accident resulted in J. B. Lenoir suffering a fatal heart attack on April 29, 1967. He was scheduled for a return to Europe later that year, having had great success there in 1965. When the news of his death spread, John Mayall, "the paternal guardian of British blues in the 1960s," recorded "The Death of J. B. Lenoir" in a cathartic response. "J. B. Lenoir is dead and it's hit me like a hammer blow," Mayall laments. Lenoir was just thirty-eight when he died. Mayall mourns the loss of a friend, but also far more: "I cry inside my heart that the world can't hear my man no more"—this man who "struggled to play an appreciated blues in vain."[7] To a certain extent Lenoir did play his blues in vain. His albums were censured by the White House. His work pales in comparison to the recognition of that received by the likes of Muddy Waters or Robert Johnson. But it still has something to say. Like an underappreciated and scorned prophet, Lenoir saw things he didn't think were right in this world and tried to sing those around him to a better place. As his tombstone's inscription says, "Let the works we've done speak for us."

Going Home

Prophets, they say, aren't welcome in their hometowns. Sometimes that's true, and sometimes it's not. Visitors to Indianola, Mississippi, are immediately struck by one overwhelming and pervasive message: This is the home of B. B. King. The claim that this is his hometown is what historians term an approximate truth. His hometown is a little plantation town that doesn't even make it onto maps, hovering somewhere between Itta Bena and Berclair, slightly east of Indianola. But the man who would become the undisputed king of the blues, born Riley B. King on September 16, 1925, called Indianola his home. Mississippi means lots of things to B. B. King. It means rows and rows of cotton fields and plantation shacks. "But above all," according to one of his biographers, "Mississippi means Nora Ella King, his mother." It also means the church. It was in the church that he learned his music, by singing with the congregation and through the rhythmic preaching, in the old Southern style, of Luther Henson, pastor at Elkhorn Baptist Church. He also heard Blind Lemon Jefferson 78s on his grandmother's Victrola. But he also remembers where he first heard the blues: "I guess the earliest sound of the blues that I can remember was in the fields while people would be pickin' cotton, or choppin' or somethin." He further confesses, "When I sing and play now, I can hear those same sounds that I used to hear as a kid." Family, church, cotton, and a guitar: the ingredients that produced the legend.[8]

King's time at Elkhorn Baptist Church was supplemented by visits to a Holiness church pastored by a distant relative, Rev. Archie Fair. He would often visit King's home, bringing his guitar with him. Fair became King's first guitar teacher. The young man immediately fell in love with the instrument but couldn't afford to buy one. Instead, he developed the instrument he had for free, his voice. Soon he laid up enough money to buy his first guitar, and though that particular one was stolen a few months later, he and his instrument of choice were inseparable. While King honed his guitar skills, America went to war. Coming of draft age in 1943, he registered and was called up. He completed his basic training, but then his plantation owner intervened. King could drive a tractor, which made him rather valuable. The owner turned over some of his crops to the military, substituting for some of his "employees." A curious moment occurs next in the life of King. German POWs were used to work the cotton fields in the South, but they had shorter workdays and were expected to bring in less cotton than the black sharecroppers were. King had always harbored a sense that things weren't right in this plantation system, and that brought his suspicions to full flower.[9] After the war, B. B. King and his guitar made their way to Memphis, where he became known as Beale Street's "Blues Boy." He landed a regular show on Memphis's WDIA, a station that was owned by whites but manned and programmed for an all-black audience. For that show, he became "B. B." King. In July 1950, he walked from Beale Street to Union Avenue and through the door of Sam Phillips's Sun Studio to make his first recordings.

King's home today is the road. As an octogenarian, he maintains a schedule of over two hundred shows a year. And every year, he returns to Mississippi. He plays at Parchman Penitentiary, where his cousin and fellow bluesman, Bukka White, served a two-year sentence. He plays in Indianola, in churches, in juke joints that were already dilapidated in the 1930s and 1940s when he learned his craft there before tired audiences of sharecroppers looking for a little enjoyment and pleasure at the end of a hard week. Indianola is the home of B. B. King, and in his stardom he has remembered to be good to his home. The town has responded in kind. The B. B. King Museum and Delta Interpretive Center opened in September 2008. It has the staples of a museum, lots of memorabilia and exhibits. It also has a stage for the blues, since this is a living tradition the museum enshrines. And it has an educational center, providing children of the Delta with the opportunities that King had to forage for on his own. B. B. King has been called many things, from King of the Blues to an international blues ambassador. He has been awarded honorary degrees from Ivy League schools, a Presidential Medal of Freedom, and multiple Grammies and industry awards. He has a spot in the Blues Foundation's Hall of Fame and in the Rock and Roll Hall of Fame. In his hometown of Indianola and throughout the Delta, he is a prophet with honor.

Among those who influenced his sound, B. B. King lists Jimmie Rodgers (not to be confused with Mississippi-born Chicago bluesman Jimmy Rogers). B. B. King recalls in his autobiography that Rodgers was a "yodeler who happened to be white, but who sang songs like 'Blues, How Do You Do?' They called him the singing brakeman and I sang along with him." In addition to being called the singing brakeman, Rogers was also known as the blue yodeler and as the father of country music. B. B. King isn't alone in naming him an influence; the Rock and Roll Hall of Fame inducted him as an "Early Influence." Early indeed, as Rodgers's time in the recording studio predated rock 'n' roll by a good two decades. Rodgers was born in Meridian, Mississippi, into a family of railroad workers. He, however, wanted to be a musician. As a mere adolescent he tried to put together a traveling music show, from which he even made some money. It all met with his father's disapproval, so it was off to the railroad.

Jimmie Rodgers worked on the New Orleans & Northeastern as a brakeman. His career came to an end in 1924, when he was diagnosed with tuberculosis, the disease popularly known as consumption, for the way it sucked the life out of its victim. Unable to work the railroads, Rodgers returned to music. Those few years on the railroad proved invaluable for his musical career. While he was traveling all through the Mississippi Delta, he heard the early bluesmen play. He no doubt even helped many of them as they hoboed around on the railroads. When Jimmie Rodgers went into the recording studio for Victor in 1927, he began a recording career that would span just seven years, during which time he battled tuberculosis and recorded 110 sides. His music evidences the blues influence, using "stock blues verses and chord progressions in his songs." "Even his trademark yodel," notes Steve Cheseborough, "may have been influenced by African American field hollers." Rodgers was influenced by these early blues, and his influence, as the gurus at the Rock and Roll Hall of Fame acknowledge, extends forward. Again, Cheseborough notes how Robert Johnson and Leadbelly often played Rodgers's songs, as did Howlin' Wolf, who modeled his trademark howl after the yodel of Rodgers. And there's the lyric.[10]

Ted Ownby from the University of Mississippi argues that while Rodgers gets credited as the father of country music, Rodgers "did not fit the mold of early country music." Ownby credits that difference to the Mississippi Delta blues, the music and musicians Rodgers met on the train. Ownby also defines that difference as Rodgers's unflinching approach to the harshness of life. Rodgers does not sentimentalize rural or farm life, as some early country music tended to do. His songs sound more like the blues, touching on the same issues: loves lost, hardships in life, and— reflecting those years as a brakeman—movement. The common thread running through each of these is Rodgers's ability to empathize. According to Ownby, Rodgers "empathized with people on the move, in large part because whether as a railroad worker or as a traveling musician, he was one of them." In Rodgers's "Hobo's Meditation," such empathy rises to the surface. The song portrays "sad men riding the trains from the point of view of a sympathetic narrator who hopes their eventual destination of heaven would have no insulting people or 'tough cops." He sang about his own suffering in "T. B. Blues." He also shows how entrenched he was in blues roots in "Mississippi Delta Blues." When these songs made their way over the radio waves, Robert Johnson, Leadbelly, and even a young Riley B. King sang with him.[11]

Jimmie Rodgers, alongside of these other blues men and women, were prophets like Moses. They identified with these oppressed people because they were of a piece with them. Further, they pointed these people, their people, to a better land waiting. But they also held out for a little justice, a little reprieve, now. Many of them had recording careers and landed tours that took them far from the Mississippi mud upon which they were born and raised. Some of them made it home often, or, as in the case of B. B. King, continued to make it home often. Some never made it back. Jimmie Rodgers died in a hotel in New York City, the tuberculosis finally getting the better of him in the middle of a recording session for Victor. J. B. Lenoir died in Illinois. None of them, however, seemed to forget those Mississippi roots. They sang to those whom they did not know, from record-company executives to European audiences, on behalf of those whom they did. They sang for the hoboes, for the sharecroppers, and for those who lost their lives in the war for civil rights. They sang of future justice. Like the prophets, they wouldn't have minded if a little of that future justice were to break into the now.

Come Sunday

These blues prophets differed, however, from their Old Testament counterparts. The prophets of the Old Testament not only looked ahead to a time of restoration, prosperity, and peace, but also looked back. And when they did, their focus was the exodus. The blues prophets couldn't point to the exodus. They found themselves either still in Egypt or suspended somewhere between the crossing of the Red Sea and the crossing of the River Jordan. In that wilderness Moses received the law, sometimes interpreted as the burden to be borne by the children of God. Yet within that law crouches the promise of grace. The command to keep the Sabbath wasn't law. It was God's gracious provision of grace. It was a blessing. There was no Sabbath in Egypt, no reprieve, no rest, no refuge. The Sabbath was a gracious provision of rest in the midst of a weary life. Over the centuries, the Sabbath came to be a crushing burden, especially by the time Jesus walked on the earth. The Sabbath became the center of petty bickering and self-righteous posturing. The religious establishment hung this once gracious promise as an oppressive millstone upon the necks of those who were in need of relief. Curiously, African American slaves regained that original intention of the Sabbath. They understood exactly what the Sabbath meant. They longed for the day of rest, for some reprieve. They longed for the freedom this grace provided. "Come Sunday," they would beg. Duke Ellington, the master of jazz, would enshrine this longing in music.

The route of Muddy Waters out of the Delta and to Chicago represents the route from the blues to rock 'n' roll. But just as Muddy Waters wasn't the only one to make the trip, so too rock 'n' roll wasn't the only child born of the blues. Jazz also had a paternal claim. The family resemblances can be heard in the sound and, again, seen in the lyric. Wynton Marsalis explains the improvisational style as not mere freehand, but as ironically programmed, orchestrated. Jazz, he says, is "harmony through conflict." He was talking about more than style. He was getting at the lyric. Jazz certainly looks like its dad.[12]

Perhaps Duke Ellington personifies the link between, as well as the journey from, blues to jazz. Born in Washington, D.C., on April 29, 1899, Edward Kennedy Ellington tottered between the worlds of the South and the North. His location provided ready access to the Atlantic seaboard musical venues, where he apprenticed by listening to the ragtime and burgeoning jazz greats. By 1923 he left the capital for New York City. The clubs, especially The Cotton Club, and the radio stations for which he played all served to make a name for Ellington, now called the "Duke," out of respect. Recording contracts and concert tours followed. By the time of his death in 1974, he had played before audiences around the globe, for kings, queens, and presidents. Though not a child of the Delta or of the Deep South, Ellington had an appreciation for his southern African American roots, evidenced in his 1943 recording *Black, Brown, and Beige.* According to the liner notes, the ink wasn't quite dry when Ellington performed this jazz suite before an audience at New York City's famed Carnegie Hall.

Ellington intended *Black, Brown, and Beige* to represent the history of African Americans, calling it a "tone parallel to the history of the American Negro." Black represents slavery, brown represents those African Americans who fought for freedom in the Revolutionary War and the Civil War, and the more complicated beige represents the ambiguities of black identity in the twentieth century. The color missing is blue, for the Duke infuses this album with the soul of the blues, especially the song "Come Sunday." "Come Sunday" started life as a wordless tune in 1943. Enlisting Mahalia Jackson, the song took on words in 1957. This version distills the sounds and the heart cry of both the spirituals and the blues. One of Ellington's biographers, Janna Tull Steed, describes "Come Sunday" as "a spiritual ballad rooted in the experience of slavery, from which sprang the bittersweet combination of present suffering, and the assurance of a promised comfort and vindication." This was a song for people stuck in the wilderness, stuck in between the promise of freedom and the realization of that promise. To call it a song is a bit misleading. It's better to call it a prayer set to music.

> Lord,
> Dear Lord above,
> God Almighty,
> God of Love,
> Please, look down,
> And see my people through.
> Come Sunday, Oh come Sunday,
> That's the day.

The words of the chorus "Come Sunday" on one level simply "mean when that day comes," like "come payday" or "come judgment day." But on another level, Sunday becomes personified. This prayer, revealing its roots in the spirituals with a reference to the exodus, not only addresses God, but also directly addresses this personified Sunday. "Come, Sunday, Oh come, Sunday," Mahalia Jackson earnestly, urgently, prayerfully pleads with a now personified day of rest. The song speaks of gray days of storm, of troubled minds and weary souls, and of tired men who've worked all day, "from dawn to sunset." And the resolution to it all lies in Sunday. That's the day when all is set right, when rest and peace and comfort descend upon weary children in a weary land. Sunday has yet another double reference. As hope had the double meaning in the blues and the spirituals of both an earthly hope and an eschatological hope, so there is both an earthly and an eschatological Sunday. Sunday in this world is the day of rest at the end of the toilsome week. Sunday in the world to come is the future Sabbath rest that awaits (Heb. 4:9).

Living in This World

When Duke Ellington included "Come Sunday" in his history of the American Negro, *Black, Brown, and Beige,* he revealed the deeply driven roots of the African American in the church. Sunday was a crucial, if not defining, piece of the African American identity. It was also a defining piece of African American music. From Muddy Waters to B. B. King, and at nearly all points in between, the blues and the men and women who sang them came from the church. Mississippi Fred McDowell offers his own take on the history of the blues, explaining that the blues comes from the reel. Anticipating that some of his listeners wouldn't know what a reel is, he continues, "You go to church, you call yourself confessing religion. Okay. Well everybody had got confidence in you, you unnerstand, that you really done confess. Well you turn around from the church song, and you start singing that. . . .

They called it a reel, you unnerstand. The blues came from the reel." The blues came from the church. The church gave these singers more than musical training. The church gave them a place to stand.[13]

"Lord, have mercy" is as much at home in a high-church prayer book as it is in the blues canon. Indeed the phrase has been nearly ubiquitous in the blues, as the previous chapters have revealed. This phrase is more than filler, more than an interpolation adding beats to hold up the line. This phrase anchors the whole genre of the blues, and it came to the blues through the church. This phrase gave the blues singers their place to stand. They knew God would be merciful, once they pled their case. They sang of floods and famines, love lost and love stolen, headaches and heartaches, hardships, troubles, and worries. They sang of these hard times, the minor key of life. That's why they call it the blues. And, ironically, they sang the blues to get the blues off of them. Mississippi Fred McDowell helps unpack this. The blues come upon you, he explains, maybe through a betraying friend or lover or some such circumstance. So you start playing, and "the more you play . . . the bluer you get, until you get to it." You play and you play and you play. And then you get "to it," you reach the point deeper than when you started, and at the deeper point you find some resolution. You've played the blues off. Or, in McDowell's words, "When I get satisfied, I put it down." McDowell's pronoun here may be referring to his guitar or to the blues or, more than likely, to both. Putting the blues down means reaching harmony through conflict; it means resolving the blues through the blues.

Harmony not only comes through conflict, but also may very well come through motion. Motion can be inspired by any number of things. It can be inspired by that pernicious rambling that got into our blood at the curse. We need to keep moving east of Eden; like predatory sharks we need to keep on the move. Motion can also be inspired by fear. Being a moving target instead of a stationary one can offer a modicum of security. Alternatively, motion can be inspired by hope. Leaving one place can spring from the desire to move to one that is better. Motion can even be motivated by a desire to act. In other words, moving from one place can also spring from the desire not simply to find a place that is better, but to make a new place that is better. This is the essence of the prophetic hope for the now. The prophet pleads his or her case precisely to exert change, to be a catalyst. That this is true, that harmony can spring from motion explains why the blues so often talks of highways and buses, railroads, and trains, theorizes James Cone. "Each," Cone informs us, "symbolizes motion and the possibility of leaving the harsh realities of an oppressive environment." He adds a proverbial saying from southern African American life to illustrate his point: "If I can just get me a handful of freight train, I'll be set." This movement also, Cone tells us, harbors "the possibility of changing the present reality of suffering." Finally, he adds, this motion reflects what writer Richard Wright calls "the endemic capacity to live."[14]

Readers of Wright's semi-autobiographical *Black Boy* are aware of how deeply Wright knew of that endemic capacity. The story chronicles a poor southern boy who, tossed about, eventually makes his way to Chicago. Before he can live, he has to survive. The main character takes up the pen to do so. Early on in the novel, Wright allows the narrator's voice to inform us that his character's desire to head north stems from his belief in justice. The main character makes his circuitous way north to Chicago. Instead of finding justice, the better place, he finds betrayal, oppression, prejudice, and a deep-seated hatred. Using physical hunger as a trope, the main character remains just as hungry in the North as in the South. In the end, that hunger is for dignity, for the affirmation of his own humanity. The hunger remains unsatisfied as the main character reaches this conclusion: "If this country can't find its way to a human path, if it can't inform conduct with a deep sense of life, then all of us, black as well as white, are going down the same drain."

But, that's not the final conclusion. The final conclusion has the narrator taking up a pencil and a blank sheet of paper, declaring, "I would hurl words into this darkness and wait for an echo, and if an echo sounded, no matter how faintly, I would send other words to tell, to march, to fight, to create a sense of the hunger for life that gnaws in us all, to keep alive in our hearts a sense of the inexpressibly human." Wright could not find a better place as he moved from one place to another, so, through writing, he set off to make one, even if it would be only a little better. Wright set off to write a better place into being. The blues artists tried to sing one into being.[15]

The blues artists, however, were not naïve optimists. Having an earthly hope and being rooted in the Sundays of this world ultimately means that the blues possesses a remarkably clear-eyed realism, avoiding altogether a naive optimism that offers saccharine answers to deeply troubling problems. "The hope of the blues," James Cones explains, "is grounded in the historical reality of the black experience." That reality was often harsh, threshing any naïveté and crushing pat answers under its weight. These artists weren't seeking an earthly utopia, a lost Shangri-La. Neither did they abandon all hope to make a change for the better. They still thought they could make a difference. Cone may be exactly right as to the grounding of this hope of the blues, but the influence of this hope transcends its roots.[16]

Bono, in an acceptance speech for the NAACP Chairman's Award, put it this way: "Poetry and righteous anger of the black American church inspired me, a white, almost pink, Irishman." Bono has applied that hope to his One Project, aimed at hunger and poverty in Africa. Bono has taken up this gargantuan task precisely because he thinks that he can make a difference. Bono finds his motivation in the poetry, in the lyric woven through the tapestry of the spirituals and the blues in the church and in the juke joints dotting the southern landscapes. He also finds the motivation in the righteous anger, a righteous anger that begat protest, and a protest that begat activism, and an activism that begat a change for the better—the genealogy of the civil rights movement that traces its roots directly to the blues. The blues has made and continues to make a difference.

Longing for the World to Come

While peace may be longed for in this world, shalom ultimately belongs to the world to come. This the spirituals knew quite well and accepted as true. Salvation would be fully realized on the other side of Jordan's shores. Consequently, the singers of the spirituals sang of that side of the shores as often as they could. Coauthors David Crowder, the musician, and Mike Hogan cleverly titled their book *Everybody Wants to Go to Heaven, but Nobody Wants to Die*. While that's true for most, some of the slaves, who were the first to sing the spirituals, saw death as a welcome end to a grim situation. When they sang of that glad morning, they were ready for it.

The spirituals are full of word pictures, taken right from the pages of the biblical prophets. There are streets of gold, pearly gates, mansions. There are vineyards and crops beyond imagination. There are robes and "walkin' shoes." Formerly tearstained eyes are now dry, and formerly empty bellies are now full and satisfied. Howard Thurman explains the significance of these word pictures in their "concreteness." This "highly descriptive language" functions to emphasize that "Heaven is a place," a place where one finds the fulfillment of all longings and aspirations. It is a place where the singer longs to be. "Swing Low, Sweet Chariot," "I'll Fly Away," "On Jordan's Stormy Banks I'll Stand," and many more spirituals show the prevalence of this theme in the spirituals. In his study of the spirituals, Bruno Chenu concludes that "the most dominant theme in them by far is that of heaven." But Chenu also warns against the mistaken conclusion that the spirituals harbored an escapism. Instead, he points to the double meaning of *heaven* in the spirituals. Heaven, like the overall eschatology of the blues and the spirituals, is both there and future *and* here and now.[17]

The spirituals gave them the opportunity to sing of heaven as a place where they would be, in words memorialized by their use in Martin Luther King's "I Have a Dream" speech:

> Free at last, free at last,
> Thank God Almighty, we are free at last.

And as they sang it, they hoped for a little freedom here on earth. These two heavens, these two hopes, are not at odds with each other; neither are they locked in some intractable tension. The reality of freedom in heaven precisely became the ground for any hope of even a modest notion of freedom in this world. Rather than foster escapism, the spirituals fostered activism. The complexity of the spirituals, laden with double references and coded meanings, reminds us to be cautious in interpreting the lyrics only on the surface. These simple rhythms and lyrics belie their subtlety and complexity. W. E. B. Du Bois captures the essence of that subtlety, the seamlessness of moving from this world to the next: "Through all the Sorrow Songs there breathes a hope—a faith in the ultimate justice of things. The minor cadences of despair change often to triumph and calm confidence. Sometimes it is faith in life, sometimes a faith in death, sometimes assurance of boundless justice in some fair world beyond."[18]

What is true of the spirituals is also true of the blues. The blues singers liked to sing of that better place down the road, and they had to keep moving on to find it. That better place may be better understood as better places. The one *there,* and the others that are *here.* Because they believed in the better place that is there, they could hold out hope, even rock-solid faith in seeing better places here.

The blues is ultimately an eschatology. As a realized eschatology, a term theologians use to speak of the ways in which the future kingdom breaks into life in this world, it has roots in the here-and-now. The blues is also a future eschatology, pointing to that world to come when the kingdom fully breaks in and returns a cursed humanity and a cursed cosmos to Eden. In his book *Everyday Apocalypse*, David Dark makes the connection between this realized eschatology and the future eschatology quite clear by looking at the very nature and meaning of the word *apocalypse*. Apocalypse, the genre of eschatology that entails the mind-spinning visions of the prophets, announces "a new world of unrealized possibility," the new world of the kingdom where the curse and its effects are eradicated. Consequently, "apocalyptic serves to invest the details of the everyday with cosmic significance." Apocalyptic further announces the kingdom in a way that the kingdom is connected, not detached, from this current world. Apocalyptic is "the place where the future pushes into the present." Dark enlists the support of scholar N. T. Wright, who makes the observation that Jesus's parables in which he teaches of the kingdom "invite listeners into a new world, and encourage them to make that world their own, to see the ordinary world from now on through this lens, within this grid. The struggle to understand a parable is the struggle for a new world to be born." The blues is an eschatology precisely in this sense of an everyday apocalypse. The blues is the struggle for the new world to come of age, the struggle to catch a glimpse of that new world in this one.[19]

The Congregation

The blues, however, is not only an eschatology. The blues is also an ecclesiology. It offers a doctrine on the life and practice of the church. The persistent image of the blues singer is of the rambling loner, that of Robert Johnson, with only his guitar as a constant companion, stealing here and there like some mysterious wind. But more often than not, even in the case of Johnson himself, blues singers were more like a pack than scattered lone wolves. When the steady stream of migrating blues singers trickled into Chicago, they looked out for one another, opened doors for one another. The music industry as a whole has been described as one in which its participants are locked in a bitter battle for survival. You eat the other's lunch before extending a hand of assistance. But these blues singers needed and fostered solidarity, not a survival of the fittest. And that solidarity extended to the audience. Mississippi Fred McDowell didn't like the term *audience*. He called the people who came to listen to him his congregation. The blues, both its singers and listeners, is a community, bound together by a truly common union of both a bitter past and present and a hope for a sweeter future.

Some of the blues singers, the ones who kept a foot in the church, had a little congregation besides their listening audiences. The Reverend Blind Gary Davis, briefly mentioned at the end of the last chapter, had many congregations. He was born in the Piedmont region in South Carolina in 1896, but he managed to get around. He started playing the blues in 1920s, adding gospel to the mix after his religious conversion in the mid-1930s. Along the way he picked up his congregations. There were those who bought his albums ever since he started recording in 1935. There were his Baptist congregations that he pastored in North Carolina, where he moved in the late 1920s, and in New York City, since his move there in the 1940s. His congregations also included the blues and folk festivals as well as the European audiences he played for in the 1960s. But if you were to ask him what congregation he most enjoyed, he would say the people he played for on the streets of Harlem. With guitar or banjo or harmonica in hand, the instruments he had played since a teenager, he wandered the streets as the blues-playing preacher.

Rev. Blind Gary Davis had remarkable longevity for a musician, with a career spanning five decades, from his first recordings in 1935 right up until his death in 1972. He is often likened to Blind Willie Johnson. But in one sense, he's a better successor to Blind Lemon Jefferson, for, like Jefferson, Gary Davis moved back and forth from the blues to the gospel, with his gospel sounding a lot like the blues and his blues overflowing with heavy doses of gospel. He could record "Cocaine Blues" in one session, only to return to the studio to record "Crucifixion" in another, a rather unorthodox minister for an unorthodox congregation on the streets of Harlem. He liked to sing of the future in heaven. In "Gonna Sit Down on the Banks of the River," he could joyfully look forward, through his scratchy, sandpaper vocals, to having a good time when we all get *there*, on Jordan's other shore. He'll meet up with those who have already passed, and he'll no longer have to say goodbye. There will be no crying there, no more lies told, no more wrongs endured, no more "troubles that I had in this world below." But while he was *here* he sang. In "I Will Do My Last Singing in This World," he vows not only to sing while he's here, but also to travel, to take his message with him. He also vows, when the words fail him, to moan while he's here, "somewhere down on my knees." And he vows to be "preachin' in this land, somewhere." He picks up this same urge in "Let Us Get Together." He calls upon his congregation to "get together/Right down here." But that's not all he expects them to do. He calls upon them, in the midst of trying times, "to do our rejoicing/Right down here." And he even expects them to "fight together/Right down here." He also adds, "Let us have our heaven/Right down here."

One of his most intriguing songs tells the story of Samson and Delilah. The song begins reminiscent of the sound of Robert Johnson's "If I Had Possession over Judgment Day." Davis begins his song with, "If I had my way," straining out three times before adding, "I would tear this building down." Davis inserts that verse throughout the song like a prizefighter unexpectedly throwing in a left hook. The song recounts how Delilah sauntered onto the scene. Rather than blame her entirely, however, Davis cleverly brings us to see how

Samson falls prey to his own devices. His strength and his accomplishments left him with a sense of invincibility, a sense that turned out to be patently false. Davis sets this portrayal of Samson's self-destruction against a backdrop of the spate of Samson's achievements. He conquered lions and whole armies, but he could not conquer his own self. All that adds a sad note to the verse that Davis constantly circles back to:

> If I had my way,
> If I had my way,
> If I had my way,
> I would tear this old building down.

As you listen you do not scorn Samson, but you become sympathetic to his frustration, you identify with his nagging limitation, a limitation that is all the more regrettable given what he is capable of and what he has accomplished. You also know that all of this serves to humble Samson. And you, too, are humbled. And you also know how the story ends. Samson's strength returns, and he tears that old building down.

Even the biblical character Jacob could be enlisted for the cause. The spiritual or folk song "We Are Climbin' Jacob's Ladder" has been recorded by such luminaries as Paul Robeson, the Staple Singers, and Arlo Guthrie. Recently, Bruce Springsteen has given the song new life through his cover of Pete Seeger's version. The song recalls the dream Jacob had, recorded in Genesis 28:10–22. Jacob, through the machinations of his mother, had just wrested his father's blessing from its rightful owner, his twin brother, Esau. At the time of the narrative of Genesis 28, Jacob is ostensibly on a journey to find a wife. In reality, he's on the run from Esau, and he's alone. One night God gives him a vision of a ladder with its base buried in the ground and its rungs stretching up to heaven. This was Jacob's promise of a way out, a promise of a means of deliverance. That promise, symbolized in the ladder, was God's covenant to Jacob, the God of Abraham, of Isaac, and of Jacob. In the dream Jacob is all alone, watching the angels move up and down the ladder. In the spiritual, the ladder becomes the ladder for *us*, for the congregation. We are on it, climbing the rungs. "We are climbing Jacob's ladder," the spiritual thunders, adding "We're brothers, and sisters, all." With every rung, the chorus rolls on, we climb higher and higher. Every rung "makes *us* stronger." We're in this together, in the struggles and in the progress. "We're brothers, and sisters, all." The song becomes a collective cry of the congregation of hope. While the song hails from the days of slavery, it has remarkable staying power. It is a song not just for slaves in that time and in that place. It was a song for the Mississippi Delta in the early 1900s. It is a song for us.

These were the sermons these spirituals and blues preachers sang and played for their congregations. They took the stories of the Old Testament, the stories of Jacob and of Samson and Moses, of David and the prophets, and they made them their own stories. They sat down next to the woman at the well, and her story became theirs. They stood as one of the crowd looking on as Lazarus came up from the grave. They watched the Man of Sorrows hang upon a tree. And they strained to help the angels roll the stone away.

The blues is a congregation of those who belong to Adam, who know what it means to be Adam and Eve's sons and daughters. It is also a congregation for whom the hope of Christ means redemption and freedom, the overturning and overcoming of that inherited curse. It is a congregation that sang and continues to sing of faith, hope, and love, one that had tasted and continues to taste the sweetness of mercy. It is a congregation that hurls their words into the darkness, listening for a faint echo in return, a congregation waiting both patiently and actively for justice as they live in this world and as they long for the world to come. The blues is a congregation that sings on Saturday night in expectation of Sunday.

Miss Del's General Store,
Clarksdale, Mississippi.

Postlude

Learning to Sing the Blues

It take a man to have the blues to sing the blues.

Leadbelly

On a cool spring evening, sitting on folding lawn chairs in the shadow of the former commissary of the Hopkins plantation outside of Clarksdale, Mississippi, a group of academics encircled a gray-haired man dressed in a fine suit, holding a guitar. Johnnie Billington had, in his earlier years, been one of any number of blues musicians who worked the cotton fields and had grown up in a cypress shack that formerly served as slave quarters on one of the Delta plantations. He was also one of many who migrated north, first to Chicago before settling down in Detroit, Michigan. Eventually he gave up music and established a business. Achieving modest success, he prepared for retirement. And then he received the call. His mother, he was told, was dying. He, unlike many who had left the Delta, returned to care for his dying mother. All this narrative was prompted by a single question asked by one in the group, "Why did you come back?"

After his mother died, Billington decided to remain in the Delta. He dusted off his guitar and formed a band, but he had to fire the members; they "were fooling around too much." In their place he recruited kids, taught them how to play instruments, and taught them some songs. They learned seven songs, which could be stretched into fourteen by staggering them for a second time through—audiences in juke joints and at parties don't always notice. Johnnie Billington had another reason, however, for recruiting these kids than simply because they would fall in line better than their adult counterparts. He tells it this way, "I wanted to put guitars in their hands instead of guns." The Delta is an economically depressed place. The two biggest employers are the casinos, plopped down along the Mississippi River, and the prisons. And in this place, Johnnie Billington wanted to make a difference—this place where he was raised by his mother and where he buried her. This place where he puts guitars in the hands of kids. And this place where he made a difference by singing the blues.

I asked him another question. I had been to Beale Street, to Clarksdale, to the site on the Stovall plantation where Muddy Waters's shack once stood, and to the Delta Blues Museum, where the reconstructed shack of Muddy Waters now meets museum patrons, complete with a wax Muddy Waters smiling over his guitar. The shack was moved there and restored by the fundraising efforts of ZZ Top, who used a spare piece from it to make a guitar they dubbed "Muddywood." And yet, despite these experiences, I still hadn't entirely found the blues. Now was my chance. So I asked him, "What is the blues?" By now Johnnie Billington had been quietly strumming chords, coaxing his guitar to life. He said without hesitation, "The blues is truth." The truth about life, the truth about *us*. He didn't use the exact words, "the human condition," but this was what he was talking about.

Pop music, that stuff on the radio, he said, was fake. It's all all right in that world, happy. When it does try to encounter sadness, he said, it just sounds plain silly. "The blues is communal," he added. "You might be okay today. Money in the bank. Tomorrow, though, you may get the blues. You'll be feeling bad. But then you hear the blues. You find out that guy up there singing, he feels bad too. And you realize that it's okay. You realize you'll get through this." Johnnie Billington helps you realize that we're all in this, the human condition, together. "The blues is living," he added again. After Katrina, Billington said, perhaps with a bit of hyperbole, 1,000 new songs arose. No, he said, shaking his head. The blues can't be pinpointed in a simple answer. The blues is alive. He then dropped down the neck of the guitar and looked straight at me. "Do you get the blues?" "No," was all I could say at the time. If I could have that moment again, I think I would say, "Not entirely, but I think I'm beginning to."

The blues is truth, the blues is community, the blues is living. The blues is the truth of the curse, the harshness that all the sons and daughters of Adam know all too well. But there is another truth that is there if you listen closely. This is the truth of grace, the truth of the cross. Singing the blues means knowing both these truths, not shrinking back or embellishing the human condition, and not failing to be an agent of grace, an agent of the one who broke into the human condition, the Man of Sorrows, who is the Truth, who is the way out, and who, through the resurrection, is the Life now and in the world to come.

The blues is community. Perhaps no one spoke of community better than Dietrich Bonhoeffer. It was Bonhoeffer who, while studying in America in 1930, pulled an ad for a Sunday school teacher off a bulletin board by a church in Harlem. At the storefront church in Harlem, Bonhoeffer heard music that he had never heard before. He left America with an armload of spirituals, and he would play those records for his students in Germany. He would listen to them as he confronted one of the most horrific powers ever to tread upon the earth. It was Bonhoeffer who spoke so clearly of the church as community, not as microcosms of disconnected individuals making a way for themselves, but as a macrocosm, a body, unified and symbiotic. The church is a community that is in this together.[1]

And the blues is living. In Memphis, Tennessee, just a few blocks north of Beale Street are the offices of The Blues Project. This has nothing to do with music. It is a medical and social services program aimed at responding to the crisis of infant mortality in that region, which ranks as the highest in the nation, a nation that boasts the premier health system in the world (though some may ask by what measure). The Blues Project may have nothing directly to do with blues music, but indirectly it has everything to do with blues music. John Coltrane, who admittedly belongs more to jazz than blues, once said, "When there's something we think could be better, we must make an effort to try and make it better. . . . It's the same socially, musically, politically." In 1960, Max Roach and Oscar Brown, Jr., would go even further; they offered a simple, two-word rallying cry, "We Insist!" The blues is an eschatology, one that offers a hope in this world and in the world to come.

In the end, the blues is not simply a music that thrived in the first decades of the twentieth century in the Mississippi Delta, then traveled north, got plugged in, and gave birth to rock 'n' roll. Its roots are in the African American experience. It flowered in the first decades of the twentieth century, after the painful sowing and cultivating that came through the decades of slavery, Reconstruction, Jim Crow, and the sharecropper system. And when the promise of a better life in the North lured many away, the blues went too. It is a music inextricably linked to the African American experience. But it is also a music for all—red and yellow, black and white. Alan Lomax recalls the moment he realized the significance of this music that he traversed the Delta to record: "As I talked to the black levee-camp workers, farmers, prisoners, mothers, and children of the delta . . . I comprehended that the music they had made out of their tribulation was becoming the music of the whole world." Though the authentic Delta blues that Lomax recorded for the Library of Congress may be gone, existing only on scratched and worn 78s, it is still a music that we must hear today. We must hear it because it teaches us an invaluable lesson. The blues teaches us what it means to be human.[2]

We tend to feel rather confident in our own selves and in our understanding of the world, our understanding of what it means to be human. We tend to be confident in our technique regarding how we live, what we value and praise, how we relate to the "other," and even in how we pray. This book has not been a book of techniques, but a book of stories and songs. These stories come from congregations in clapboard churches, from aspiring musicians living in shotgun shacks on cotton plantations looking out upon row after outstretched row of cotton. These stories are told from the porches of general stores and commissaries, from the juke joints off gravel roads where music plays all night long, and from the dazzling lights on Beale Street in Memphis. The tellers of these stories offer us their songs, their blues. And if we let them, these storytellers will also teach us to sing the blues.

Discography

This list offers a place to start to listen to the blues. I have arranged these selections by corresponding chapters in the book. The more ambitious collectors may wish to consult Robert Santelli, *The Best of the Blues: The 101 Essential Albums* (New York: Penguin, 1997).

Chapter 1

Blues Masters, The Essential Blues Collection: Volume 8, Mississippi Delta Blues, Rhino, 1993.

Mississippi: Saints & Sinners: From before the Blues and Gospel, the Deep River of Song series, Rounder, 1999.

Chapter 2

Robert Johnson, *The Complete Recordings*, Columbia Records/Sony Music Entertainment, 1990.

Muddy Waters, *The Complete Plantation Recordings: The Historic 1941–1942 Library of Congress Field Recordings*, MCA Records, 1993.

Muddy Waters, *The Anthology*, Chess/MCA Records, 2001.

Chapter 3

Charlie Patton, *Primeval Blues, Rags, and Gospel Songs*, Yazoo Records, 2005.

Son House, *Delta Blues: The Original Library of Congress Sessions from Field Recordings 1941–1942*, Biograph Records, 1991.

Chapter 4

Blind Willie Johnson, *The Complete Blind Willie Johnson*, Columbia Records/Legacy, 1993.

Blind Lemon Jefferson, *The Best of Blind Lemon Jefferson: Classic Recordings of the 1920s*, Yazoo Records, 2000.

Bessie Smith, *The Collection*, Columbia Records, 1990.

Ma Rainey, *Ma Rainey's Black Bottom*, Yazoo Records, 1991.

Chapter 5

Thomas A. Dorsey, *Precious Lord: The Great Gospel Songs of Thomas A. Dorsey*, Sony 1994.

Soundtrack, *O Brother, Where Art Thou?* Lost Highway/Mercury, 2000.

Mississippi Fred McDowell, *"I Do Not Play No Rock 'n' Roll,"* EMI-Capitol Music, 2000.

Mississippi John Hurt, *Avalon Blues: The Complete 1928 OKeh Recordings*, Columbia/Legacy/Sony Music Entertainment, 1996.

Chapter 6

B. B. King, *Singin' the Blues/The Blues*, Virgin Records, 1993.

Reverend Gary Davis, *Pure Religion and Bad Company*, Smithsonian Folkways, 1992.

Duke Ellington, *Black, Brown, and Beige: Duke Ellington and His Orchestra, Featuring Mahalia Jackson*, Columbia/Legacy/Sony Music Entertainment, 1999.

Jimmie Rodgers, *The Essential Jimmie Rodgers*, RCA Records, 1997.

Notes

Chapter 1 What Hath Mississippi to Do with Jerusalem?

1. Tertullian, *De praescriptione hereticorum* [On the Rule of the Heretics], 7. H. Richard Niebuhr identifies Tertullian as a supreme example of the "Christ against culture" view. "Doubtless," Niebuhr writes, "the greatest representative in early Christianity of the 'Christ-against-culture' type was Tertullian." See *Christ and Culture* (New York: Harper, 1951; reprint, 2001), 51. Niebuhr's typology of views on the church-and-culture problem also includes Christ of culture, Christ above culture, Christ and culture in paradox, and Christ the transformer of culture. This exploration of the blues intends to fit the last category.

2. See Dietrich Bonhoeffer, *Letters and Papers from Prison*, ed. Eberhard Bethge (New York: Simon & Schuster, 1997), 339–42 and 369–70; James H. Cone, *The Spirituals and the Blues* (Maryknoll, NY: Orbis, 1991); Jon Michael Spencer, *Blues and Evil* (Knoxville: University of Tennessee Press, 1993), xxi. See also Spencer's *Theological Music: An Introduction to Theomusicology* (Westport, CT: Greenwood Press, 1991). One further example of theomusicology is Rodney Clapp's "The Glorious Mongrel: How Jazz Can Correct the Heresy of White Christianity" in his *Border Crossings* (Grand Rapids: Brazos, 2000), 185–202.

3. Paul Oliver, "Blues," *The New Grove Dictionary of Music and Musicians*, 2nd ed., vol. 3, *Baxter to Borosini*, ed. Stanley Sadie (New York: Grove's Dictionaries, 2001), 730.

4. "Match Box Blues" would later be covered by Carl Perkins (1951) and Bob Dylan (1994). Blind Lemon Jefferson's 1927 recording was by OKeh, the classic "race records" label. For an essay on the technical analysis of the blues, see Graeme M. Boone, "Twelve Key Recordings," in *The Cambridge Companion to Blues and Gospel Music*, ed. Allan Moore (Cambridge: Cambridge University Press, 2002), 61–88.

5. William Banks Taylor's *Down on Parchman Farm: The Great Prison in the Mississippi Delta* (Columbus: Ohio State University Press, 1999) documents the checkered past of Parchman Prison. Illinois Central Railroad material is cited in James C. Cobb, *The Most Southern Place on Earth: The Mississippi Delta and the Roots of Regional Identity* (Oxford: Oxford University Press, 1992), 98.

6. Alan Lomax, *The Land Where the Blues Began* (New York: New Press, 1993), 405–22. See also Robert Gordon, *Can't Be Satisfied: The Life and Times of Muddy Waters* (Boston: Little, Brown, 2002).

7. For both "The Negro Speaks of Rivers" and a selection from *The Ways of White Folks*, see Langston Hughes, *Vintage Hughes* (New York: Vintage, 2004).

8. Cobb, *Most Southern Place on Earth*.

9. For a detailed account of the region's ecology and history, see Mikko Saiku, *This Delta, This Land: An Environmental History of the Yazoo-Mississippi Floodplain* (Athens: University of Georgia Press, 2005); and Robert Gordon and Bruce Nemerov, *Lost Delta Found: Rediscovering the Fisk University–Library of Congress Coahoma County Study, 1941–1942* (Nashville: Vanderbilt University Press, 2005).

10. Clifford Geertz, *The Interpretation of Cultures* (New York: Basic Books, 1973). Bobby Blue Bland, personal interview, March 14, 2006.

11. John C. Willis, *Forgotten Time: The Yazoo-Mississippi Delta after the Civil War* (Charlottesville: University Press of Virginia, 2000). For a discussion of cotton and the Delta economy, see Clyde Woods, *Development Arrested: The Blues and Plantation Power in the Mississippi Delta* (London: Verso, 1998). Woods argues that the sharecropping system left an already disadvantaged people group even more so and that the harshness of life gave rise to the blues. His book further treats the troubling economy of the present-day Delta. The Johnny Cash lyric is from "The Ballad of Barbara."

12. See Kevin Kenny, *Making Sense of the Molly Maguires* (Oxford: Oxford University Press, 1998).

13. Cone, *Spirituals and the Blues*. See also Earl L. Stewart's discussion of spirituals in *African American Music: An Introduction* (Belmont: Thomson, 1998), 21–38; and Jerma A. Jackson, *Singing in my Soul: Black Gospel Music in a Secular Age* (Chapel Hill: University of North Carolina Press, 2004), 8–26.

14. With an extensive prehistory, the arrangement of most contemporary versions of "Stormy Monday" may be credited to T. Bone Walker.

15. W. C. Handy, *Father of the Blues: An Autobiography* (1941; reprint, Da Capo Press, 1991), 7–8. "Yellow Dog Blues," as Handy titled it, plays off two railroads in the Delta. The Southern Railway and the Yazoo Delta Railroad were colloquially termed the Yellow Dog (nobody seems to know exactly why).

16. Johnny Cash with Patrick Carr, *Cash: The Autobiography of Johnny Cash* (New York: Harper Collins, 2003), 7.

17. Johnny Cash, *At Folsom Prison* (Sony Music, 1999).

18. Steve Turner, *The Man Called Cash: The Life, Love, and Faith of an American Legend* (Nashville: W Publishing Group, 2004), 139. Cash, depending on the occasion, could offer numerous reasons as to why he wore black. His identification with the oppressed, however, is the one reason that he put in song.

Chapter 2 I Be's Troubled

1. Robert Gordon, *Can't Be Satisfied: The Life and Times of Muddy Waters* (Boston: Little, Brown, 2002), 43–44. For Lomax's discussion of the moment, see *Land Where the Blues Began* (New York: New Press, 1993), 417–18. See also Robert Gordon and Bruce Nemerov, eds., *Lost Delta Found: Rediscovering the Fisk University-Library of Congress Coahoma County Study, 1941-1942* (Nashville: Vanderbilt University Press, 2005) for a discussion of Work's ethnographic and ethnomusicological study of the Delta and field notes.

2. Keith Richards, "Foreword," in Gordon, *Can't Be Satisfied,* xi.

3. Chess Records, Muddy Waters's label, was located on Maxwell Street in Chicago, literally at the end of Highway 61, the route out of the Delta. The success of "I Can't Be Satisfied," according to Nadine Cohodas, "had turned Leonard [Chess, who co-owned the label with his brother Phil]

into a blues believer." *Spinning Blues into Gold: The Chess Brothers and the Legendary Chess Records* (New York: St. Martin's Griffin, 2000), 51–52.

4. John Milton, *Paradise Lost*, bk. 10.

5. Elijah Wald, *Escaping the Delta: Robert Johnson and the Invention of the Blues* (New York: Amistad, 2004). And for fuller discussions of the disputed resting place of Robert Johnson see John Hammond's DVD *The Search for Robert Johnson*. The character Tommy Johnson in the Coen brothers' *O Brother, Where Art Thou?* is based on both Robert Johnson and blues legend Tommy Johnson (1896–1956), who, like Robert Johnson, claimed to have sold his soul to the devil for his talents.

6. Robert Santelli, *The Big Book of Blues: A Biographical Encyclopedia* (New York: Penguin, 2001), 253.

7. Wald, *Escaping the Delta*, 109.

8. Steve Cheseborough, *Blues Traveling: The Holy Sites of Delta Blues*, updated 2nd ed. (Jackson: University Press of Mississippi, 2004).

9. Ibid., 113–14; "Hellhound on My Trail," recorded June 20, 1937.

10. Alfred Encarnacion, "Bulosan Listens to a Recording of Robert Johnson," in *Blues Poems*, ed. Kevin Young (New York: Knopf, 2003), 183.

11. For Johnson's recorded songs, see *Robert Johnson: The Complete Recordings*. The liner notes contain the lyrics.

12. For the Legba myth and the world of the Delta Blues, see Jon Michael Spencer, *Blues and Evil* (Knoxville: University of Tennessee Press, 1993), 28–34.

13. Liner notes, Eric Clapton, *Me and Mr. Johnson*.

14. Wald, *Escaping the Delta*, 178, 267.

15. "Cross Road Blues" also contains the words, "tell my friend-boy Willie Brown," which is a tribute to the musical influence of Son House and Willie Brown.

16. Nadine Cahodas, *Spinning Blues into Gold: The Chess Brothers and the Legendary Chess Records* (New York: St. Martin's Griffin, 2000), 44, 40.

17. Muddy Waters, "Five Long Years."

18. Cited in Gordon, *Can't Be Satisfied*, 128; Muddy Waters, "Cold Up North" and "My Home Is in the Delta."

19. Langston Hughes, *The Ways of White Folks* (New York: Vintage, 1990), 33–49.

20. Marva Waters, cited in Gordon, *Can't Be Satisfied*, 266; Muddy Waters, cited in Gordon, 284.

21. Jon Michael Spencer, *Blues and Evil*, 55. Compare Muddy Waters's lyric to that of Son House in "Preachin' the Blues Part 1," recorded May 28, 1930: "Oh and I had religion, Lord this very day / But the womens and whiskey, well they would not let me pray"; or to the lyric of Furry Lewis in "Mistreatin' Mama," recorded August 28, 1928: "I could have religion, Lord this very day / But the womens and whiskey, Lord won't let me pray."

22. Spencer, *Blues and Evil*, 54; Muddy Waters citation in Gordon, *Can't Be Satisfied*, 32.

23. Dietrich Bonhoeffer, *Dietrich Bonhoeffer Works*, vol. 3, *Creation and Fall*, ed. John W. de Gruchy, trans. Douglas Stephen Bax (Minneapolis: Fortress, 1997), 120.

24. Ibid., 144.

25. Cornelius Plantinga, Jr., *Not the Way It's Supposed to Be: A Breviary of Sin* (Grand Rapids: Eerdmans, 1995).

26. Henry Townsend cited in Paul Oliver, *Conversation with the Blues* (New York: Horizon, 1965), 170; W. E. B. Du Bois, *The Souls of Black Folk*, centennial ed. (New York: Modern Library, 2003), 192.

Chapter 3 Man of Sorrows

1. Santelli, *Big Book of Blues: A Biographical Encyclopedia* (New York: Penguin, 2001), 220.

2. Son House, "Walking Blues."

3. David Evans, liner notes, *Son House: Delta Blues and Spirituals*, 7.

4. Alan Lomax, *Land Where the Blues Began* (New York: New Press, 1993), 259.

5. Bruce Rosenberg, *Can These Bones Live? The Art of the American Folk Preacher* (Chicago: University of Illinois Press, 1988), uses Rubin Lacy as exemplar of the rhythmic preaching style.

6. David Evans put his birth at 1881 in *Big Road Blues: Tradition and Creativity in the Folk Blues* (New York: Da Capo, 1982), 175. In a later publication, Evans came to argue that "Patton was almost certainly born in 1891." Michael Taft suggests 1887 in *Talking to Myself: Blues Lyrics, 1921-1942* (New York: Routledge, 2005), 469; while Robert Santelli holds to 1891 in *Big Book of Blues*, 370.

7. See John M. Barry, *Rising Tide: The Great Mississippi Flood of 1927 and How It Changed America* (New York: Simon & Schuster, 1998).

8. Stephen Yafa, *Cotton: The Biography of Revolutionary Fiber* (New York: Penguin, 2005), 237.

9. David Evans, liner notes, *Screamin' and Hollerin' the Blues*.

10. William Ferris, *Blues from the Delta: An Illustrated Documentary on the Music and Musicians of the Mississippi Delta* (New York: Doubleday, 1978), 28.

11. W. E. B. Du Bois, *The Souls of Black Folk*, centennial ed. (New York: Modern Library, 2003), 192.

12. J. I. Packer, "The Gospel Bassoon," *Christianity Today*, October 28, 1996.

Chapter 4 Woman of Sorrows

1. André LaCocque, *Ruth: Continental Commentaries* (Minneapolis: Fortress, 2004), 144.

2. Todd Linafelt has argued for the poetic structure and rhythm of Naomi's speech in "Ruth," *Berit Olam: Studies in Hebrew Narrative and Poetry* (Collegeville, MN: Liturgical Press, 1989), 17–21. With apologies to my Old Testament scholar friends, I've simply taken it one step further in calling it a blues. Dietrich Bonhoeffer, *Meditations on the Cross*, ed. Manfred Weber, trans. Douglas W. Stott (Louisville: Westminster John Knox Press, 1999), 86. Ida Goodson quotation from *Wild Women Don't Have the Blues*, a film by Christine Dall (San Francisco: California Newsreel, 1989).

3. Allen Dwight Callahan, *The Talking Book: African Americans and the Bible* (New Haven: Yale University Press, 2006), xi, 20; Wilma Anne Bailey, "The Sorrow Songs: Laments from Ancient Israel and the African American Diaspora," *Yet with a Steady Beat: Contemporary U.S. Afrocentric Biblical Interpretation*, ed. Randall C. Bailey (Atlanta: Society of Biblical Literature, 2003), 61, 83.

4. Paul Oliver, *The Story of the Blues* (Boston: Northeastern University Press, 1997), 41; Blind Willie McTell, "Dying Crapshooter's Blues."

5. For a brief discussion of Blind Willie Johnson, see Mark A. Humphrey, "Holy Blues: The Gospel Tradition," *Nothing But the Blues: The Music and the Musicians*, ed. Lawrence Cohn (New York: Abbeville Press, 1993), 119–26.

6. For a brief treatment of the life of Blind Lemon Jefferson, see Samuel Charters, *The Blues Makers* (New York: Da Capo, 1991), 175–89.

7. Samuel Charters, *The Poetry of the Blues* (New York: Avon, 1963); Paul Oliver, *The Meaning of the Blues*; Angela Y. Davis, *Blues Legacies and Black Feminism: Gertrude "Ma" Rainey, Bessie Smith and Billie Holiday*

(New York: Pantheon, 1998), 97; Hermann Gunkel, *Introduction to the Psalms: The Genres of the Religious Lyric of Israel* (Macon: Mercer University Press, 1995), 86–91.

8. Kirsten Nielsen, *Ruth*, trans. Edward Broadbridge, Old Testament Library (Louisville: Westminster John Knox Press, 1997), 52.

9. Katharine Doob Sakenfeld, *Ruth*, Interpretation: A Biblical Commentary for Teaching and Preaching (Louisville: John Knox Press, 1989), 81–82.

10. Sandra R. Lieb, *Mother of the Blues: A Study of Ma Rainey* (Boston: University of Massachusetts Press, 1981), 130.

11. Angela Y. Davis, *Blues Legacies and Black Feminism*, 128.

12. Sterling Brown, "Ma Rainey," *The Collected Poems of Sterling A. Brown*, ed. Michael S. Harper (New York: Harcourt, Brace, 1932).

13. Christopher John Farley, "Bessie Smith: Who Killed the Empress?" in *Martin Scorsese Presents the Blues: A Musical Journey* (New York: Amistad, 2003), 104–11.

14. Sidney Bechet cited in Henry Louis Gates, Jr., and Cornel West, "Bessie Smith," *The African American Century: How Black Americans Have Shaped Our Country* (New York: Free Press, 2002), 109; Mahalia Jackson cited in Christopher John Farley, "Bessie Smith," *Martin Scorsese Presents the Blues*, 105.

15. Angela Y. Davis, *Blues Legacies and Black Feminism*, 97; Buzzy Jackson, *A Good Woman Feeling Bad: Blues and the Women Who Sing Them* (New York: W. W. Norton, 2005), 68; Ralph Ellison, *Shadow and Act* (New York: Vintage, 1972), 257. Reams have been written about the controversy/conspiracy surrounding her death. See Elaine Feinstein, *Bessie Smith* (New York: Viking, 1985), for a comprehensive treatment.

16. Hilton Als, "Billie Holiday," *Martin Scorsese Presents the Blues*, 114.

17. See Philip Dray, *At the Hands of Persons Unknown: The Lynching of Black America* (New York: Modern Library, 2003).

18. Jack Schiffman cited in David Margolick, *Strange Fruit: The Biography of a Song* (New York: HarperCollins, 2001), 76–77.

19. Etta James and David Ritz, *Rage to Survive: The Etta James Story* (New York: Villard Books, 1995), 264.

20. Mark A. Humphrey, "Holy Blues," 125.

Chapter 5 Precious Lord

1. Thomas Dorsey is not to be confused with, neither is he related to, the brother team of big band leaders Tommy and Jimmy Dorsey.

2. Don Cusic, "The Development of Gospel Music," *The Cambridge Companion to Blues and Gospel Music*, ed. Allan Moore (Cambridge: Cambridge University Press, 2002), 53.

3. Howard Thurman, *Jesus and the Disinherited* (New York: Abingdon-Cokesbury Press, 1949), 11, 16–19.

4. Obery M. Hendricks, Jr., *The Politics of Jesus: Rediscovering the True Revolutionary Nature of Jesus' Teachings and How They Have Been Corrupted* (New York: Doubleday, 2006), 76; Allan Dwight Callahan, *The Talking Book: African Americans and the Bible* (New Haven: Yale University Press, 2006), 238–39; James H. Cone, *The Spirituals and the Blues* (Maryknoll, NY: Orbis, 1991), 44.

5. Michael W. Harris, *The Rise of the Gospel Blues: The Music of Thomas Andrew Dorsey in the Urban Church* (New York: Oxford University Press, 1994), 47.

6. Ibid., 65–67.

7. Ibid., 68.

8. The citation is in Giles Oakley, *The Devil's Music: A History of the Blues* (New York: Taplinger, 1977), 116.

9. Cone, *Spirituals and the Blues*, 46.

10. For these and more examples of this identification with the character from the biblical text in the spirituals, see Bruno Chenu, *The Trouble I've Seen: The Big Book of Negro Spirituals* (Valley Forge, PA: Judson Press, 2003), 159–62.

11. James "Kokomo" Arnold, "Mean Old Twister Blues," 1937.

12. Stanley Crouch, "The Afrocentric Hustle," *City Journal*, Summer 1994 (4:3).

13. See John Donne's poem, "Good Friday, 1613. Riding Westward."

14. Rev. Gary Davis, "Death Don't Have No Mercy."

15. I am grateful to Martin Luther and to Mark Husbands for this idea of God's yes against our no. I read it in Luther. I did not find it in print by Husbands but heard it from him in a prayer he offered during one of the sessions of the Wheaton Theology Conference in 2006. More fundamentally, see 2 Cor. 1:18–21.

16. Cone, *Spirituals and the Blues*, 49.

17. Callahan, *Talking Book*, 240–41.

18. Chenu, *Troubles I've Seen*, 162.

19. Cone, *Spirituals and the Blues*, 52.

20. Mississippi Fred McDowell in liner notes to *Mississippi Fred McDowell: "I Do Not Play No Rock' n' Roll"* (EMI-Capitol, 2001); Alan Lomax, *The Land Where the Blues Began* (New York: New Press, 1993), 328.

Chapter 6 Come Sunday

1. Both citations are from David Evans, *Big Road Blues: Tradition and Creativity in the Folk Blues* (New York: Da Capo, 1982), 18.

2. John Lee "Sonny Boy" Williamson, aka Sonny Boy Williamson #1, and Aleck Miller, aka Rice Miller and aka Sonny Boy Williamson #2, were not related. The first was born in Jackson, Tennessee, in 1914. The second was born in Glendora, Mississippi, in 1910. Robert Santelli explains the origin of the #1 and #2. Sonny Boy Williamson #1's "stature was such that Rice Miller, a great blues harmonica player who followed in his path, assumed Williamson's name as his own, presumably both to capitalize on Sonny Boy #1's fame and to carry on his legacy." *The Big Book of Blues: A Biographical Encyclopedia* (New York: Penguin, 2001), 518.

3. Paul Oliver, *Conversations with the Blues* (New York: Horizon, 1965), 29.

4. Santelli, *Big Book of Blues*, 237. For brief sketches of Sonny Boy Williamson #1 and #2, see Santelli, 518–21, and David Evans, *The NPR Curious Listener's Guide to Blues* (New York: Perigee/Penguin, 2005), 162–64.

5. Robert Santelli, *The Best of the Blues: The 101 Essential Albums* (New York: Penguin, 1997), 261. Santelli includes two albums from Lenoir in his coveted list, ranking at numbers 65 and 83.

6. John Perkins, *Let Justice Roll Down* (Ventura, CA: Regal Books, 1976), 21, 154–58.

7. Santelli, *Big Book of Blues*, 319.

8. Sebastian Danchin, *"Blues Boy": The Life and Music of B. B. King* (Jackson: University Press of Mississippi, 1988), 2, 5.

9. Ibid., 9.

10. Steve Cheseborough, *Blues Traveling: The Holy Sites of Delta Blues*, 2nd ed. (Jackson: University Press of Mississippi, 2004), 190.

11. Ted Ownby, "Jimmie Rodgers: The Founder of Country Music," *Mississippi History Now*, July 2004.

12. See "Freedom of Expression with a Groove: An Interview with Wynton Marsalis," in *Jazz: A History of America's Music*, ed. Geoffrey C. Ward and Ken Burns (New York: Knopf, 2000), 116–21.

13. Mississippi Fred McDowell, liner notes to *Mississippi Fred McDowell: "I Do Not Play No Rock 'n' Roll,"* EMI-Capitol, 2001.

14. James Cone, *The Spirituals and the Blues* (Maryknoll, NY: Orbis, 1972), 124–25. The citation from Wright is from the foreword to Paul Oliver, *The Meaning of the Blues* (New York: Collier Books, 1963), 9.

15. Richard Wright, *Black Boy*, 60th anniv. ed. (New York: HarperCollins, 2005), 383–84.

16. Cone, *Spirituals and the Blues*, 124.

17. Howard Thurman, *Deep River and The Negro Spiritual Speaks of Life and Death* (Richmond, IN: Friends United Press, 1990), 48; Bruno Chenu, *The Trouble I've Seen: The Big Book of Negro Spirituals* (Valley Forge, PA: Judson Press, 2003), 211.

18. W. E. B. Du Bois, *The Souls of Black Folks*, centennial ed. (New York: Modern Library, 2003), 264.

19. David Dark, *Everyday Apocalypse: The Sacred Revealed in Radiohead, the Simpsons, and Other Pop Culture Icons* (Grand Rapids: Brazos, 2002), 11–13; Wright, cited in Dark, may be originally found in *Jesus and the Victory of God* (Minneapolis: Fortress, 1996), 176.

Postlude Learning to Sing the Blues

1. Dietrich Bonhoeffer, *Life Together* (New York: Harper, 1978).

2. Alan Lomax, *The Land Where the Blues Began* (New York: New Press, 1993), 327–28.